The Malayan Emergency

NIAS – Nordic Institute of Asian Studies
New and recent Monographs

NIAS Press is the autonomous publishing arm of NIAS – Nordic Institute of Asian Studies, a research institute located at the University of Copenhagen. NIAS is partially funded by the governments of Denmark, Finland, Iceland, Norway and Sweden via the Nordic Council of Ministers, and works to encourage and support Asian studies in the Nordic countries. In so doing, NIAS has been publishing books since 1969, with more than two hundred titles produced in the past few years.

UNIVERSITY OF COPENHAGEN

 **norden**

Nordic Council of Ministers

THE MALAYAN EMERGENCY

A Small, Distant War

Souchou Yao

The Malayan Emergency
A Small, Distant War
by Souchou Yao

Nordic Institute of Asian Studies
Monograph series, no. 133

First published in 2016 by NIAS Press
NIAS – Nordic Institute of Asian Studies
Øster Farimagsgade 5, 1353 Copenhagen K, Denmark
Tel: +45 3532 9501 • Fax: +45 3532 9549
E-mail: books@nias.ku.dk • Online: www.niaspress.dk

A CIP catalogue record for this book is available from the British Library

ISBN: 978 87 7694 190 1 (hbk)
ISBN: 978 87 7694 191 8 (pbk)

Typeset in Arno Pro 11/14.15
Typesetting by Donald B. Wagner

Printed and bound in the United States
by Maple Press, York, PA

Contents

Illustrations

Preface

A friend, a distinguished anthropologist at Harvard, once pronounced in an email, 'I don't do social science anymore.' His latest book recounts the pleasure and intellectual influence from a lifetime's reading – Kafka, Jorge Luis Borges, Italo Calvin, Edna St Vincent Millay, Ted Hughes. I don't have his fame, or his decades-long appointments in universities across three continents. But I admire his disciplinary verve, and his generosity in showing us a fresh way of unearthing the meanings and significance of a human event.

Anthropology is an empirical craft. Its emphasis on fieldwork and ethnography keeps our feet on the ground; theoretical generalization is built upon the social reality in 'my village' or 'my neighbourhood'. The discipline is evolving. For some practitioners, there is an urgent need to break free from the stricture of social science with its neat prescription of proposition, evidence and final resolution. Works like Shamus Rahman Khan's *Privilege: The Making of an Adolescent Elite at St. Paul's School*, and Christine J. Walley's *Exit Zero: Family and Class in Postindustrial Chicago*, for example, illustrate that sociological truth can be garnered from using a freer range of sources and methods: personal memoirs, auto-ethnography, novel-like micro descriptions, in addition to interviews and fieldwork. Apart from my own inclination, *The Malayan Emergency* is an attempt to pitch a tent on the field of the innovative and methodological turn taking place in anthropology and its sister disciplines.

Historians and defence study experts have given us detailed and thoughtful accounts of the Malayan insurgency. My contribution is to take the reader, after surveying the trees, to the forest – the postwar conditions facing Great Britain, the strategic calculations of the late British Empire, the social and political circumstances in Malaya, the chancy (mis)calculations of the Empire and the Malayan Communist Party. It seems to me right to stress that to understand the 'why' and 'how' of the Malayan Emergency, these factors mattered; not just the Templer leadership and the British genius of imperial policing. I also believe that a project such as this should ease ourselves into a position of moral judgement. To ape a Maoist saying, the Emergency is a not a dinner party; it was so full of violence, imperial greed and political fantasy that very few facts about the conflict can be left unread and unreinterpreted.

We share the burden of historical hindsight. Working on the book, I have been struck with unease when young academics and activists have shown a bare awareness of another 'people's revolution' in the region that was the harbinger of communism's social and moral catastrophe. The Khmer Rouge's murderous work took place in the then Kampuchea almost next door to us in Malaysia and Singapore. However, it is a hard task to evaluate the undertakings of the Malayan – or any – communist movement, not the least because of our own intellectual and ideological wills. For me, this evaluation is not about evoking the Cold War demonization of communism; it certainly should not mean giving over to nostalgia for a revolution and its unrealized ideal. The famous adage of 'history in its own context' is a useful guide. What happened in the past is best examined in its own time and context. Yet, philosophical speculation, which fosters the view of the general case, helps to enrich our understanding that human behaviours observe a pattern, a universal narrative, that traverses the past and the present. 'It happens here, too. And it happens as well in our time.'

The book is peppered with the sense of futility, of times lost, as felt by the ex-insurgents I encountered. Yet, even as I share their melancholy, I do not forget the forces of the hope for justice that communism once inspired. Until the signing of the German–Soviet Non-Aggression Pact in August 1939, communism seemed to many to be the only serious opposition to Fascism. Young communists like Cheng Peng and Xiao Hong did not talk about the Hitler–Stalin 'friendship'. If they knew of it, it would not have dampened their dream of a socialist utopia in Malaya. My telling of the life-careers of Xiao Hong and Second Cousin is indication enough, I imagine, of how seriously I perceive the importance of communism to the young people of their respective generations.

THIS BOOK WAS WRITTEN in Sydney, Australia and Port Dickson, Malaysia, with research bolstered by visits to Singapore and Thailand. Professor Chua Beng Huat hosted a presentation of my early thinking on the subject at the Asian Research Centre, National University of Singapore. In Singapore I was put up, in grand hospitality, by Desiree Hüls and Leo Biezeman, whose friendship and presents of Oolong Tea made lighter the writerly task. Thanks also to Gerald Jackson for his positive words, and to Alan D'Cruz, J. Kuna Rajah Naidu and Geraldine Moores for their encouragement and assistance.

Souchou Yao
Port Dickson, Malaysia

Malaya at the time of the Emergency. (Sources: various. Forest cover 1962 based on material in Jeyamalar Kathirithamby-Wells, *Nature and Nation: Forests and Development in Peninsular Malaysia*, NIAS Press, 2005.)

1 On Empire
A sleek and orderly retreat

There have been many great empires in history... There is only one Empire where, without external pressure or weariness at the burden of ruling, the ruling people has voluntarily surrendered its hegemony over subject peoples and has given them their freedom.
– Clement Attlee, British Prime Minister (1945–51)

The principles [of Victorian world strategy] had been distilled from a century and more of accumulated experiences, from far-reaching and varied experiments in the uses of power to promote trade and in the uses of trade to promote power.
– Ronald Robinson and John Gallagher, *Africa and the Victorians* (1982)

I t has been called many things: 'the orderly management of decline', 'transfer of power', 'the great ship going down'.[1] They all describe the British Empire's last gasp in the first decade after the Second World War, before its final sunset with the withdrawal from 'East of Suez' in 1968. For empire apologists, these phrases were sorely needed to express what they saw as Britain's postwar realism and paternal responsibility to its colonies. No longer, even they recognized, was Britain a world power, and its interests now were mostly limited to Europe and the North Atlantic. The British Empire was dismantling and Britain would, with grace and beneficence, transfer power to its colonial subjects. Historian Jack Gallagher has called this the narrative of 'the great ship' going down, 'without convulsion, without tremor and without agony'.[2] It is an

---

1   For the sources of these phrases, see Bernard Porter, 'Trying to make decolonisation look good', *London Review of Books* 29(15), 2007, pp. 6–10.
2   John Gallagher and Anil Seal, *The Decline, Revival and Fall of the British Empire*, Cambridge: Cambridge University Press, 1982, p.153.

image dripping with nostalgia: the graceful old battleship, presided over by her long-serving captain and seamen, being ceremoniously scuttled to rest in the deep. We in Malaysia have long been fed with a similar idea of the Empire; not so much a retired battleship as a dignified, well-mannered guest who knows when to leave and not to overstay the welcome. Malaya may well be a textbook case of 'good' British decolonization. When Britain withdrew in 1957 after more than two hundred years of colonial rule, it left a healthy economy, a Westminster system of government and a stable, peaceful multi-ethnic society, after fighting a costly war against communist insurgents. But, the Empire's goodwill was evident in other parts of Asia. In a series of withdrawals, it had earlier granted independence to India and Pakistan (August 1947), Burma (January 1948) and Ceylon (February 1948). Indeed, as decolonization rolled on like an unstoppable wave, Britain seemed to be managing it with skill and prodigious good sense.

Britain had a considerable success in selling to the world its rhetoric of decolonization. It had become something of a legend that Britain was so much more civilized when it came to shedding colonies than, say, France with Algeria or Holland with the Dutch East Indies. In truth, the divestment of the British Empire was, in many cases, neither orderly nor peaceful. In the case of Asia, even its early departures from India and Burma – often cited as examples of Britain's goodwill in granting independence – were messy and bloody. The partition of India displaced more than twelve million people and left hundreds of thousands dead, and newly independent Burma found itself in a state of civil war. Indeed, 'Nowhere down the length of the [Southeast Asian] crescent,' historians Christopher Bayley and Tim Harper write, 'did relinquished or devolved British authorities pass quietly into the hands of a homogeneous nation-state.'[3] Notably too, the two decades after the end of the Second World War may have been times of decolonization, but they also saw the invasion of the Suez Canal and in the remaining colonies, mandated territories and places of 'spheres of influence' the Empire was busily reasserting itself and against the graceful retreats from India, Burma and Ceylon, there were counter-insurgency wars in Kenya (1952–56) and Cyprus (1952–59), and intervention in Palestine (1947–48) and notoriously in the Greek Civil War (1946–49) with the aim of holding on to a strategic foothold in the Mediterranean. Instead of decolonization and the waning of the Empire, the opposite seemed to be hap-

---

3   Christopher Bayly and Tim Harper, *Forgotten Wars: Freedom and Revolution in Southeast Asia*, Cambridge, Mass.: Harvard University Press, 2007, p. 188.

pening. But for all the complexities and circumstances of these conflicts, there was a global pattern and a matching of timelines in the events. In Malaya, after the withdrawal from Palestine many policemen came and served in Britain's other insurgency in the tropics, bringing with them their experiences of dealing with Arab and Jewish terrorists; and the Malayan Emergency that started in June 1948 eventually provided a blueprint for the anti-Mau Mau campaign in Kenya four years later. Instead of divestment of Empire, Britain seemed to be holding on, as it went about protecting its interests and the trappings of a Great Power. The postwar period of imperial retreat turned out to be one of intense military activity.

To the historian Bernard Porter much of Britain's divestment of Empire was about 'making decolonisation look good'.[4] This was done, he suggests, by way of showing the reverse of what actually took place: rather than as something forced upon Britain by its decline, the liquidation of the Empire had been in fact a sign of strength and wisdom. Many believed that decolonization was a logical culmination of centuries of imperial rule which had given Britain a special 'cultural sensitivity' to the colonized peoples and their aspirations. In fact, Porter argues, Britain's retreat from the colonies was largely due to the inevitability of the end of Empire, an inevitability 'so blindingly obvious to all save the most abject blimps' who included 'some leading politicians – Churchill initially, and Ernest Bevin'.[5] Porter writes,

> [Historically] the empire had been 'overstretched' for a long time: run on a shoestring and with very few personnel, inadequately defended by a second-rate military, and with little domestic commitment to it, especially if it involved sustained repression. Its eventual collapse should thus come as no surprise. . . . All it needed . . . was a serious 'Western' challenge, and a wholesale withdrawal of the indigenous collaboration that had helped sustain the empire . . . [6]

Postwar realism did not mean the wholesale abandonment of Empire, however. A more nuanced approach is to see the postwar decolonization as highly selective and strategic. On the imperial chessboard key moves were thus made: while some territories were to be let go, others were stubbornly held on to at least until conditions were deemed right for the transfer of power, after

4 Porter, 'Trying to make decolonisation look good'.
5 Ibid., p. 7.
6 Ibid., p. 2.

British interests had been secured. What happened was something like the streamlining of Empire in the postwar conditions, when financial and troop commitments hung heavily over the chambers in Whitehall. Concerning Malaya, we might even speak of a kind of 'cost and benefit analysis' in the British decision to fight the insurgency. In India, say, where, in order to maintain the imperial hold on a subcontinent of nearly 400 million people, huge security forces and exorbitant financial resources would have been needed to quash political discontent and rising violence. By comparison the decision to defend the Southeast Asian colony won hands down in terms of both costs and economic return. Malaya was worth fighting for.

IT IS A CHARMING fluke of history that the start of the communist insurrection in Malaya and, far away in Europe, the Berlin airlift to feed the besieged city in Soviet-occupied East Germany took place a month apart in the same year, 1948. Thus, the echoes of the Cold War were heard in Malaya as those in government circles began to talk about fighting 'a Moscow-directed insurgency'. Peking was also mentioned, as was the fact that the guerrillas were mostly Chinese who allegedly owed their loyalty to China. This turned out to be an ideological fantasy.[7] Neither Moscow nor Peking had a hand; no arms from foreign powers flowed to the Malayan jungle. Yet in 1948 many British officials saw the trouble in Malaya as a part of a communist plan for world domination. The Director of Operations in Malaya, Lt. General R. H. Bowen, wrote in a secret report:

> The Malayan Communist Party campaign is part of a wider Soviet-inspired drive to obtain control of what is strategically and economically one of the most important areas of South-East Asia. ... In June 1948, on the instruction of the Cominform issued at two conferences in Calcutta four months earlier, the MCP started a campaign of murder, sabotage and terrorism designed to paralyse the Government and develop into armed revolution.[8]

The idea of an Asian Cold War, and local insurgencies receiving Soviet instruction through the conduit of the Communist Information Bureau (Cominform) also dominated the mind of the Attlee Labour government. Arthur Creech Jones, the British secretary of state for the colonies, believed the MCP

---

7   See, for example, Phillip Deery, 'Malaya, 1948: Britain's Asian Cold War?', *Journal of Cold War Studies* 9(1), 2007, pp. 29–54.

8   'Review of the Emergency in Malaya', ibid., p. 34.

was 'the nerve centre of the whole subversive movement', and the colonial office was sure that there were 'substantial grounds for regarding the Malayan outbreak as stimulated by Moscow'.[9] Historians have since put the idea to rest. But 'the Malayan insurrection as Moscow-directed conspiracy' made sense at the time. It came about because Britain needed an explanation for its actions in Malaya that could cut through the maze of internationalism, anti-colonialism and national self-determination that defined the struggle in the colonial world at the time.

Postwar Britain was keen to be seen as an international power which would play its part in the anti-communist crusade. Britain's sense of vulnerability began in the world war just ended. For all of Churchill's 'we shall fight on the beaches' resoluteness of 1940–41, it was realized that British survival would depend on the charity of its major ally, the United States. Eventually the US entry to the war, and later Stalin's prodigious willingness to spill the blood of his soldiers as they pursued Hitler's forces from the Eastern Front to the Battle of Berlin, had come to win the war and save Britain.[10] During the Cold War the US role was similarly crucial: in providing leadership, strategic vision, manpower and above all material from its industrial might. There is something else: a Britain committed to the Cold War would help to mollify the US resentment of its Empire, and serve to press the point that Washington should perhaps once again bankroll a British war.

However, before the outbreak of the Korean War in June 1950, the Cold War was still very much a focus of Europe. In mid-1948 the Iron Curtain had slammed down fast and the eleven-month Berlin Blockade had begun; in Czechoslovakia, a Soviet-engineered coup had replaced the democratically elected government with one dominated by communists. Against the haunting spectre of another European conflict, struggles in Malaya, the Dutch East Indies, Burma and Indochina were lost in the distant, misty East. In any case, unlike Europe, Washington was dragging its feet, unwilling to be drawn into a region considered primarily a French and British sphere of influence.[11] It was dead set on not getting bogged down in helping European powers hold on to their colonial possessions.

---

9 Ibid.

10 Max Hasting, for example, sees the Battle of Stalingrad through the winter of 1942–43, not the Allied D-Day landing in Normandy in June the following year, as the turning point of the Nazi defeat in Europe. See his *Armageddon: The Battle for Germany 1944–45*, London: Macmillan, 2004.

11 See Deery, 'Malaya, 1948: Britain's Asian Cold War?', p. 31.

Thus, it was that in June 1948, four days after the launching of the Malayan Emergency, the Malayan deputy commissioner of police met with the US Consul in Kuala Lumpur. He asked for assistance, including ten thousand US Army small-calibre carbines – light infantry rifles suited for jungle warfare – and two million rounds of ammunition. The US consul turned him down. The deputy commissioner should go to the right authorities, the Malayan Chief Secretary, he said.[12] An incident such as this made clear, not only to the despondent police chief, that the US would not help. In the Malayan conflict, Britain was on its own. It had to find its own means, its own justifications, for fighting what turned out to be a very costly war.

MALAYA, BRITAIN'S RELUCTANT COLONY, had proved its economic worth in the closing years of the 1800s. For centuries the Malays had known of the deposits of alluvial tin in the west of the peninsula, though they mined little of it. Chinese immigrants came and, like the Malays, worked on deposits close to the surface, but using a simple and effective method of washing the gravel to extract the tin. Soon larger operators with capital and machines began to move in. When European investors started to arrive at the end of the eighties, they brought new technology in the form of high-pressure hoses and steam pumps that washed out the ore and extracted it from the sludge; and from 1912, the more efficient bucket dredges that dug deep into the watery depth were brought to Malaya. From the first discovery of rich tin fields in 1848, in the course of a few decades a new and alien economy spread across the western foothills of Perak and Selangor and Negri Sembilan, notably in the vicinity of modern Taiping, Ipoh and Kuala Lumpur.[13] At the end of the nineteenth century, Malayan tin exports totalled more than half of the world output and Singapore was a major centre for the smelting of tin ore.

The early twentieth century blessed Malaya with another vital industrial commodity. The world demand for rubber was led by its use in electrical wire and motorcar tyres, the Ford Model T began mass production in 1909, reaching its peak at the end of the 1930s. The British had brought rubber seeds from Brazil, and successfully germinated them in the tropical-plant house at

---

12 'Discussion of Present Situation in Malaya with Government Authorities', Report presented to the Secretary of State, Kuala Lumpur, 28 June 1948; ibid., p. 33.

13 A good account of the history of tin mining in Malaya is Francis Loh Koh Wah, *Beyond the Tin Mines: Coolies, Squatters and New Villages in the Kinta Valley, c. 1880–1980*, Singapore: Oxford University Press, 1988.

Kew Gardens in London, and at the Singapore Botanic Gardens under its director Henry Nicholas Ridley. Ridley was an energetic promoter of rubber, nick-named 'Mad Ridley' for his enthusiasm. The success of the rubber planting owed much to his vision and scientific skill. When rubber seedlings were transplanted in Malaya in 1877, they thrived in a climate and soil conditions very similar to those found in Brazil's rain forests. Like tin, rubber became Malaya's industrial fortune, and soon replaced tin as its top export. By 1955, two years before independence, Malaya's rubber exports were worth $1,584.5 million Malayan dollars.[14]

I grew up with the story of tin and rubber, and had drummed into my mind the wise British rule and economic foresight, the visionary Englishman Ridley, the Chinese and Indian labourers who toiled in the mines and plantations, the final transformation of Malayan society and economy. But this is really two stories in one. For the arrival of tin and rubber also witnessed the rapacious grab for power by Britain.

Historically Malaya was associated with the goods of ancient trade – birds' feathers, edible birds' nests, aromatic woods, some gold and tin; and from the 1850s onwards, with tapioca, sugar, coffee, pepper and gambier resin (for tanning and dyeing). In contrast, the new commodities hauled us into modern industrial capitalism. To Britain, Malaya was no longer a possession of doubtful viability, but a 'real estate' of vast financial wealth. For the first time the need to protect and assist its advancement became a crucial concern. From the expansion of tin mining in the 1870s, to the rise of rubber in the early 1900s, to the commodity boom of the two world wars, the period turned out to be one of consolidation of power.

The British Empire after the Tudors was founded on the Far Eastern trade. It was built on a chain of trading posts protected by strategically placed naval bases. Malaya, which includes the peninsula and the island of Singapore at the south, lies at the 'inner lake' of the South China Sea. The west coast faces the narrow Straits of Malacca, and trading ships had passed through here on the way to and from China and India for centuries. Not surprisingly, European empires vied to control the Malayan western seaports. Trade and profit were key, but during the Napoleonic Wars (1803–15) the British intervention was also motivated by fear of French designs on the East. After the dust of imperial rivalry had settled, at the

---

14 Federation of Malaya, Annual Report, 1955, quoted in Charles A. Fisher, *South-East Asia: A social, economic and political geography*, London: Methuen, 1964, Table 82, p. 693.

opening of Queen Victoria's reign in 1837 Britain was in possession of a fortified trading town (Malacca, since 1825), and two harbours and naval bases along the west of the Peninsula (Penang and Singapore, acquired in 1786 and 1819, respectively). Administratively these became the Straits Settlements, formal colonies ruled from London. These were prosperous seaports; the hinterland, in contrast, was mostly jungle. The aborigines inhabited the highlands, and the Malays ruled by petty chiefs and sultans had founded settlements along the coasts and beside rivers. The Malay rulers were often in strife with one another. The expansion of tin mining intensified the rivalry, as the sultanates competed for tax revenues from the mines. At the same time, Chinese labourers began to flood into the tin-rich river valleys along the west coast, bringing with them their social divisions and secret societies. Social chaos and violence disrupted trade and industry, and drove home to the British that to control the Straits Settlements the rest of the peninsula had to be brought under administrative rule. London had to step in, and the result was the installation of British Residents and Advisers in Malay courts in return for British protection. By 1874, less than three decades after the discovery of the rich tin fields of Perak, Britain had gained control of the whole of the Malay Peninsula.

As the twentieth century got underway, British rule in Malaya was a system of baroque complexity. The Straits Settlements were formal colonies; the Federated Malay States – Selangor, Perak, Negri Sembilan and Pahang – were British protectorates, which took 'counsel' from the Residents and the Resident General, later the Chief Secretary of the Federation; the rest of the territories formed the Unfederated Malay States which were also British protectorates, though they came under the Advisers. But constitutional niceties can a bit of a red herring. Although the Malay States were not colonies, the courts were treaty-bound to accept the advice of the Residents or Advisers 'on questions other than those touching on Malay religion and custom'. In any case, the arrangement gave Britain near absolute power. The complex colonial structure of the Straits Settlements and the Malay States lasted until the end of the Second World War. It could not survive the Japanese occupation and the loss of British prestige and was dissolved in 1946. By then new political conditions and a new ideological climate had arrived that would change forever the foundation of British rule.

THIS SMOOTH-RUNNING NARRATIVE FROM tin and rubber to colonial power can oversimplify, though. The reality was more convoluted. It was John Robert Seeley, classical scholar and son of a Christian Evangelist, who famously wrote, commenting on the British Empire of the eighteenth century, 'We seemed . . .

to have conquered and peopled half the world in a fit of the absence of mind.'[15] It is a beguiling saying – a most quotable quote – about the unplanned, slipshod way in which Britain acquired its overseas territories. Certainly Malaya had been a reluctant addition to the Empire. The acquisition of the colonies that eventually formed the Straits Settlements was motivated by the fear that another European power would take the seaports if Britain didn't. Protection of trade was a concern, so was imperial rivalry. By 1874 the Napoleonic Wars had long ended, and although Russia showed no sign of extending the Great Game in Eurasia to the East, possible incursion of another European power was very much on Britain's mind. *Realpolitik* as much as imperial imaginings held sway, along with trade and economic interests.

The Colonial Office was staffed by hard-nosed men pragmatic about the costs and gains of maintaining an empire. They kept a tight rein on the budget. For all the talk of imperial prestige, they eschewed direct military conquest and intervention, and they expected the colonies to pay their way. The result was 'world domination on the cheap'. In 1898, when the Empire's naval bases dotted the globe from Halifax in the North Atlantic to Wellington in the Southern Ocean, the total defence budget was slightly more than £40,000,000, a mere 2.5 per cent of net national product.[16] Budgetary discipline could hardly be aligned with a hit-or-miss approach to the affairs of Empire.

All the same, there is something in Seeley's idea. For one thing, it seems to reflect how the Empire had actually worked. From London's perspective, there were so many schemes promoted out in the world by overzealous officials, so many 'not to be missed opportunities' cooked up by amateur imperialists, all seeking the government's interest. Whitehall's approach was more prudent and cautious, lest it be burdened with a territory financially and politically costly. Malaya illustrated Whitehall's wisdom. In hindsight British action in Malaya was sensible and politically astute: the acquisition of the Straits Settlements had protected trade; the intervention in the Malay states had restored peace and order desired by all – even the bellicose Malay rulers. At the time, however, it didn't look quite like this on the ground.

The problem was distance, which gave considerable freedom to the 'man on the spot'. Singapore had been less a calculated move of Empire than the personal vision of one man, a former clerk at the East India Company's head

---

15 Niall Ferguson, *Empire: How Britain made the modern world*, London: Penguin Books, 2003, p. 248.

16 Ibid., p. 247.

office in Calcutta. Raffles saw the island as a place of trade and strategic importance, but it lay within the Dutch sphere of influence. The exchanges of letters between Singapore and London each took ten months, and at that distance the Foreign Secretary could be forgiven for thinking that Raffles was motivated more by personal ambition than by Singapore's potential benefits to Britain. After all, another 'upstart', Captain Francis Light, in 1786 had given Britain the island of Penang, which proved neither profitable nor suitable for ship repair or fitting. As for the Malay states, matters developed so rapidly that *local* British officials often needed to act and interpret their instructions with dispatch. In 1873, Sir Andrew Clarke, the Governor of the Straits Settlements, received from the Colonial Office the instruction that he was to 'influence' the Malay states, 'with a view to rescue, if possible, those fertile and productive countries from the ruin which would befall them if the present disorder continued unchecked'.[17] The counsel of prudence – that 'if possible' – did not prevent the Straits Settlements from being involved in the dispute of a royal succession, the suppression of Chinese secret societies, and a punitive war against Malay rebels after the murder of a British Resident. The Royal Marines steered rather than 'influenced' the enforcement of treaties with the Malay states.

The idea of the British Empire as somehow imposing its will on the world with public school insouciance – Niall Ferguson's *Empire: How Britain Made the Modern World* makes much of it; Jeremy Paxman in the BBC television series *Empire* can't help mentioning it – is in one way bunk. But it is also not far from expressing anxiety about the imperial project itself: the vast territories of formal and informal colonies, their remoteness, the need for troop commitments to quell rebellions and protect borders, and always the financial costs and what Britain could get out of it. When Britain found itself being drawn deeper and deeper into the affairs of the Malay Peninsula, the concerns of Empire were both grave and realistic. For if political entrenchment were made *a fait accompli*, the Empire would find it hard to extricate itself.

BRITISH MALAYA WAS SAVED by tin and rubber, and not only in the economic sense. In many ways Malaya fitted well with the image of a colony pressed upon Britain by circumstances. The rivalry between European imperial powers, the politics of the Malay states, the initiatives of men like Light and Raffles, the arrival of immigrants and its social-economic effects – they all play a part in the

---

17 Paul H. Kratoska, *South East Asia, Colonial History: Empire-building in the nineteenth century*, London: Routledge, 2001, p. 255.

making of Empire in Malaya. More than anything, it was these circumstances that gave the acquisition of Malaya a tinge of 'adventurism'. Tin and rubber, it is not too much to say, settled the issue of Malaya as a colony of dubious value. The idea of British strategic interest was given a solid, material footing, investing in the imperial undertaking a new purpose and economic rationale. As Britain brought the peninsula under control, tin and rubber would eventually make it a jewel of British possession in Southeast Asia. With that knowledge, Britain knew what it needed to do and why it should stay when at the end of the Second World War it was challenged by an anti-colonial movement of some force and legitimacy.

Empire and its wars were never only about territories, oil and minerals, or trade. Prestige and influence were also crucial. Such prestige and influence made for the 'soft power' that glazed over the skin of imperial might. As British indirect rule drew on local customs and traditions, imperial 'soft power' would articulate itself in the spheres of the culture and psychology of both the ruler and the ruled. This is the point of George Orwell's majestic *Shooting an Elephant*: the need of a colonial official to 'impress the natives' on the white man's competence and superiority.[18] However, it is easy to forget that imperial prestige would also operate in the more mundane affairs of finance and trade.

Unlike, say, Raj India, Malaya with its dense jungle, its simple people and immigrant labourers had brought no special glory to the British Crown. It is hard to imagine a writer like William Dalrymple getting excited about the place. At the mention of Malaya, no castle-dotted plain or wind-swept desert comes to mind, but rather the sweat-glistened faces of coolies, the swirl of smoke from smelting plants, and the whamming and cranking of machines in rubber sheet pressing sheds. On the other hand, Malaya was a colony palpable, patent of trenchant material benefits in the way Raj India or Aden could not be. The romance of Malaya, such as it was, could only be told with the dry, droning discourse of economic theory.

IN 1897, THE YEAR of Queen Victoria's Diamond Jubilee, the British Empire occupied a quarter of the world's surface, putting more than 400 million people under some form of British rule. But imperial power was not only in the expanse of territory and the size of population under rule, but also in Britain's financial reach. At the opening of the twentieth century, Britain held a large proportion

---

18 George Orwell, 'Shooting an Elephant', *The Collected Essays, Journalism and Letters of George Orwell*, vol. 1, Harmondsworth, England: Penguin, 1968.

of its assets overseas, and two-fifths of these were capital investments abroad, then valued at £3.6 billion. About half of these were in the British colonies. As its importance and profitability grew, the Empire attracted some 44 per cent of portfolio investment from British and foreign interests. At the same time, the colonies were receiving increasing volumes of British exports – in 1902 two-fifths of the Empire's imports came from Great Britain. On this side of the ledger, then, much favoured the island nation. But the uncomfortable fact is that Britain was importing more than it was exporting. This it could well afford as the deficits were paid for by its huge earnings from investments overseas. In any case, in the condition of free trade, British export prices enjoyed a 10 per cent term of trade over import prices; in short, each dollar earned from exports enabled Britain to purchase one-tenth more the value of imports.[19]

In these transactions, investors, importers and exporters needed a reliable currency. To grease investment and trade, the preferred currency had to keep its value and the rate of exchange with other currencies could not wildly fluctuate; trust and stability were crucial. In 1868, only Britain, Portugal, Egypt, Canada, Chile and Australia were on the gold standard. With the gold standard and as a global power, Britain set the standard for the international monetary system. The pound sterling ticked the boxes on trust and stability because it was the currency of an Empire of economic and military might. The gold standard meant that the value of the paper notes was backed by gold: each pound sterling carried the an equivalent value in gold, and the Bank of England guaranteed that paper notes could be 'sold' for gold.[20] The pound sterling became the currency of global trade.

In September 1931 Britain abandoned the gold standard, which had been made unsustainable by a couple of factors. The United States had since 1900 backed the greenback with gold. Since then the dollar had been gradually eating into the position of the pound, as people shifted to the currency of this rising industrial power. At the same time, the Great Depression caused people to distrust paper money and currency holders rushed to exchange sterling for gold. In this situation the Bank of England faced a real prospect of the depletion of its gold reserve, and a threat to Britain's financial solvency itself.

In place of the gold standard, Britain established in September 1939, the time of the German invasion of Poland, the sterling area.[21] The currency un-

---

19 Ferguson, *Empire*, p. 240–244.

20 en.wikipedia.org/wiki/Gold_standard. Accessed 13 February 2015.

21 en.wikipedia.org/wiki/Sterling_area. Accessed 13 February 2015. See also Hugh Gaiskell, 'The Sterling area', *International Affairs*, 28(2), 1952, pp. 170–176.

ion – for that's what it was – included the colonies and the dominions, except Canada and Hong Kong. A wartime emergency measure, it was also a sign of the waning of the British Empire as it turned to the generosity of the colonies. The arrangement required the member states to peg their currencies against the pound, instead of gold or the US dollar. By then Britain had itself moved to back sterling with mainly the greenback, and less with gold and silver. The centre of world monetary system had substantially shifted. What this meant was that for sterling area countries their export foreign earnings – mainly in dollars – would be deposited at the Bank of England and converted into the sterling that each member state needed to back its own paper currency. These deposits became, in effect, obligatory loans of the colonies to the Empire. The Bank became a trading house of dollars for sterling, and a holder of foreign reserves of sterling block members. The arrangement pooled gold and foreign currency reserves of all member countries to help Britain finance the war and support the pound. In 1944, Britain entered into the Bretton Woods managed exchange rate system which gave the pound a fixed exchange value against the dollar. But the exchange rate was set too high for such a ruined economy. In 1949 Britain reluctantly devalued the pound by 30 per cent, leading to huge losses in the sterling area member nations.

The real story of the fall of the pound is the decline of the British Empire. Britain had for too long drawn on its financial clout and imperial prestige, but by the end of the Second World War both were in short supply. The history of the pound tells of Britain's attempt to assert its diplomatic and financial weight above its real capabilities. Since the value of the pound was regarded as a direct reflection of Britain's international standing, the sterling exchange rate had often been set unsustainably high. For a long time, Britain resisted the devaluation of the pound because it would, in the words of economist Robert Carbaugh, 'indicate a failure of domestic policies and a loss in international prestige'.[22] Domestic policies and the politicians' agenda were one thing; international factors also dictated the fortune of the nation's currency. For a major power like Britain, international confidence was everything. Investors and sterling holders had to believe that the pound would hold its value, that it would be used safely as a reserve currency, and that it would purchase the amount of British goods importers desired. The value – the international acceptance – of the pound was ultimately tied to the power and prestige of the

---

22 Robert J. Carbaugh, *International Economics*, Mason, USA: South Western Cengage Learning, 2008, p. 455.

British Empire. The Indian diplomat Krishnan Srinivasan says as much when he writes: 'International confidence in sterling seemed to depend on Britain acting as a great imperial power'; and he argues that the 1956 invasion of the Suez Canal was launched because Nasser's 'piracy on the Canal posed a great danger to sterling'.[23] British military actions, it can be said, aimed to protect the Empire as much to safeguard the value of the pound.

BY 1957, THE YEAR Malaya was given independence, the communist insurgency was all but broken. Fighting the Emergency had been hugely expensive. From 1948 until its departure Britain sank huge resources and manpower into the conflict. The armed forces reached their peak in 1952, when the British deployed some 40,000 British and Commonwealth troops, 67,000 police and special constables, and more than 250,000 Home Guards.[24] An official estimate put the overall costs at £700 million, to which the UK government contributed £520 million or more than 70 per cent. In 1951 alone, the war cost £69.8 million – £56 million borne by British taxpayers and the rest by the Malayan government.[25] These were significant figures given the state of the British treasury at the time. After their victory in the first postwar election, the new Labour government had begun nationalizing the key industries – from the Bank of England and civil aviation to iron and steel and electricity and gas – and put in measures to create the welfare state. All this brought spiralling costs to a government already financially strained. As Sir Henry Tizard, one of Prime Minister Attlee's chief advisers, spoke about the pressing economic woes: 'We are a bankrupt nation. It will tax our strength and determination in the next years to provide for our necessary imports by exports. Until we succeed we shall only keep alive through the charity of our friends.'[26]

To meet the costs of the Emergency, Britain would borrow heavily from the United States, and from the colonies and the dominions through their contribution of dollar earnings to the sterling block. Three years earlier, in 1945, when the war ended, Britain's liability was fifteen times greater than what it

---

23 Krishnan Srinivasan, *The Rise, Decline and Future of the British Commonwealth,* London: Palgrave Macmillan, 2005, p. 72.

24 Karl Hack, 'Everyone lived in fear: Malaya and the British way of counter-insurgency', *Small Wars & Insurgencies,* 23(4–5), 2012, p. 671.

25 Nicholas J. White, 'Capitalism and counter-insurgency? Business and government in the Malayan Emergency, 1948–57', *Modern Asian Studies,* 32(1), 1998, p. 176.

26 Deery, 'Malaya, 1948: Britain's Asian Cold War?', p. 32.

could afford to pay back from its reserve. This liability included debts incurred to sterling area members as well as their deposits held at the Bank of England. Postwar Britain was a nation of crushing foreign debt.

All this helps to explain the anomaly of the Empire at its twilight. At a time when it was busily withdrawal from its overseas territories, aggressive military actions were launched to protect what remained. As for the Malayan Emergency, like the invasion of the Suez Canal, it had the appearance of economically inspired adventurism at a time when the Treasury could barely afford to pay its bills.

Yet, despite the talk of Britain as a bankrupt nation and the need to 'go begging from friends', imperial prestige never totally lost its purchase. Historically imperial prestige had led to the overevaluation of the pound by a government that refused to accept the decline of the currency as a part of the costs of fighting the First World War. The devaluations of 1930 and 1949 were reluctant moves considered compromising to the viability of the Empire. However, the idea of imperial prestige as Britain's 'financial booster' should not be taken too far. Even after the Second World War, when the Empire was at its lowest ebb, there was no short age of nostalgia for Britain's imperial achievements. Churchill and some in the Labour government thought it worth preserving, and a revamped Empire based on the key strategic positions in Asia and the Mediterranean would affirm Britain's new international role. Then there was the Cold War. When the renewal of the Empire led to fighting communist insurgencies, it showed the West, particularly the US, that Britain was doing its bit in protecting freedom and democracy. Imperial prestige was cherished for its own sake; it could win allies and restore some of Britain's past glory.

Malaya made for a special case in the idea of the greatness of Empire and its economic significance. Malaya's economic importance to Britain makes us see the Emergency with a more pragmatic eye. The counter-insurgency was very much a bread-and-butter war for the Empire. The idea haunted inner government circles. A British Lord expressed the sentiment of the time when he told Parliament, '[Malayan businesses] have largely supported the standard of living of the people of this country and the sterling area ever since the war ended. What we should do without Malaya, and its earnings in tin and rubber, I do not know.'[27] Perhaps alone among the colonies, Malaya, a place that inspired no imperial glory, had given the war-weary British people a better life, a more viable economic future.

---

27 Mark Curtis, *Web of Deceit: Britain's Real Foreign Policy*, London: Vintage, 2003, p. 335.

The speaker might have had in mind the hard figures. In 1950, at the height of the communist insurrection, Malaya's exports – mostly rubber and tin – were worth US$226 million, and the Korean War boom the following year brought the figure to US$406 million. From 1948 to 1950, Malaya contributed US$650 million to the sterling area reserve; Malaya remained the biggest dollar earner among all the Commonwealth nations throughout the fifties.[28] But the colony's economic value to Britain rested not only on dollar earnings. Owing to the heritage of Empire, Britain held substantial business assets in the peninsula: some 70 per cent of the rubber estates were owned by British firms. Creech Jones, the secretary of the colonies, was candid about Malaya's importance to the Empire. As he told the Cabinet in July 1948: '[Malaya] is by far the most important source of dollars in the colonial empire and it would gravely worsen the whole dollar balance of the Sterling Area if there were serious interference with Malayan exports.'[29]

This talk about Malaya as 'Britain's saviour' is telling. Rubber and tin were important not only in the way of rescuing Britain from its financial woes, but also in eliciting a type of imagination and fantasy. 'What we should do without Malaya' might well have articulated in the British mind a tangled set of ideas and feelings: the desire for what the commodities delivered; the need to keep Malaya within the imperial hold; the fear of losing the colony and its wealth. Unforgettably and alluringly, a cultural gloss was put on the mundane products of Malaya. In the process, tin and rubber began to take on a heightened sense of expectation about what they were and what they could do. There is something in the British pronouncements that lurches toward Marx's idea of commodity fetishism:

> A commodity is ... a mysterious thing, simply because in it the social char-
> acter of men's labour appears to them as an objective character stamped
> upon the product of that labour; because the relation of the producers to
> the sum total of their own labour is presented to them as a social relation ...
> between the products of their labour. [With commodities] the existence of
> the things qua commodities, and the value relation between the products
> of labour which stamps them as commodities, have absolutely no connec-
> tion with their physical properties and with the material relations arising

---

28 Catherine R. Schenk, *Britain and the Sterling Area: From Devaluation to Convertibility in the 1950s*, London: Routledge, 1994, p. 25.

29 Quoted in John Darwin, *Britain and Decolonisation: the Retreat from Empire in the Postwar World*, London: Macmillan, 1988, p. 138.

therefrom. There it is a definite social relation between men, that assumes, in their eyes, the fantastic form of a relation between things. [30]

In Marxist terms, commodity fetishism is simply the highest expression of the 'bewitchment' of rubber and tin to which even the most hard-headed British officials were not entirely immune to absolutely. From disciples of Marx, the Australian Communist Party, in a 1951 pamphlet entitled 'Leave Them Alone! Malaya Must Cost No More Australian Blood!', declared:

> Mincing Lane is the remote throne of the Malayan rubber empire. . . . The Australian investment, chiefly controlled by the Collins House monopoly group is worth about £25 million and the Goodyear Rubber Co., had investment in both Malaya and Indonesia.
>
> The men of Mincing Lane in London and Collins House in Melbourne don't tap rubber under the equatorial sun, but they toil hard in the lobbies of Westminster and Canberra. Any threat to Malaya's riches – and the guns bark, the lash descends on the jail yards.[31]

Sounding hoarsely rough-hewn, the statement nonetheless carries a flawless sociological reasoning. The real issue about rubber, so the sentiment goes, is about monopoly capitalism and its cosy relationship with Westminster and Canberra. As owners of the Malayan rubber industry, 'the men of Mincing Lane and Collins House' would lobby the state for the protection of their assets – a rendering of the classic 'the state as the handmaiden of the capitalist class' argument. Much of this is instrumentalist, vulgar Marxism. However, Marx's phrase 'the social character of men's labour' takes us to the very conditions in which rubber and tin were produced. And these conditions would certainly encompass the colonial political structures –imperial rule itself – that 'assisted' the production and profit-making of industries. In the language of commodity fetishism, tin and rubber are so full of significance, so invested with meaning and desire, that we lodge them in phenomena and processes to which we affix the words 'culture' and 'imagination'. The end statement of the pamphlet is suggestive of this: 'Any threat to Malaya's riches – and the guns bark, the lash descends on the jail yards.' I urges the

---

30 Karl Marx, Capital, vol. 1 [1867]: trans. S. Moore and E. Aveling in *The Marx-Engels Reader*, ed. R. C. Tucker, 2nd edn, New York, W. W. Norton, 1978, pp. 320-1.

31 Rupert Lockwood, *Malaya must cost no more Australian blood*, Sydney: Current Book Distributors, 1951, p. 4. Australian troops were a part of the Commonwealth forces that fought in the Emergency.

reader to consider the violent rapidity of response, the punishing measures, the psychological fear, when the colony's wealth was threatened. Marx's idea of commodity fetishism, I believe, is an important supplement to the argument about the financial significance to Britain of Malaya's major exports. Imperial prestige and military action had, however circuitously, attempted to support the pound sterling. But as 'commodities', tin and rubber complicate considerably the totality of reasons for explaining Britain's decision to fight a counter-insurgency war in Malaya.

WRITING ABOUT THE EMERGENCY, one is struck by the 'symptoms' of an empire in decline. Britain had prided itself on being a nation of shopkeepers; its overseas ventures were nursed in the glasshouse of free trade and liberalism. Niall Ferguson can talk about 'How Britain made the modern world', to quote the subtitle of his book *Empire*. But the world under imperial rule was one in which the sense of splendour and progress was outweighed by the miseries it caused. To understand the nature of Empire and its effects requires much more hardy intellectual labour than Ferguson has offered. Works like *Empire* and Jan Morris's *The Pax Britannica Trilogy* are full of charming descriptions, and it takes a keen eye to see beyond the exotic, entertaining tales to the moral shambles of imperial rule. For Ferguson the Empire is defensible for the good it did for the colonized people. For me the most endearing justification of Empire is still the idea of a Noel Coward-type insouciance that supposedly characterized British actions overseas. It is not difficult to see the point: the Empire moulded by a haughty casualness suggests the marvel of its power and the genius of its builders. However, as with all fantasies, it needed only the lightest touch to show up its gaping insubstantiality, like applying a wet finger to a paper lantern.

In Malaya, the achievement of the Empire in retreat had been bloody and pragmatic. Even with the postwar conditions of decolonization, the British undertaking in Malaya was calculated and carried out with a strong political will. The aim was to restore British authority, and to rebuild the colonial economy after its devastation by the Japanese occupation. When the Emergency began in June 1948, after an initial setback British resolve never wavered. The marriage of imperial prestige and the colony's earning power, we might say, provided the men in Whitehall with commitment and clarity of purpose in regard to Malaya. When Britain left in 1957 it marched out in triumph: imperial prestige was restored, its economic assets were secured by the country's pro-British, market-friendly government. Some of us, though, cannot help noticing the irony. For those who have read the literature, Malaya may come across as culturally banal. Yet, if the colony did not increase the heartbeat of imperial enthusiasts, it was Empire's rustic possession in Southeast Asia that kept Mother Britain from the poor house. This may well be the Emergency's most telling historical significance: it opens up the British actions in Malaya to the inner contradictions and moral pretensions of Empire.

2 On Communism
New Person in a New Era

Communism was modernity's most devout, vigorous and gallant champion.
– Zygmunt Bauman, 'Living Without An Alternative' (1991)

Every act of rebellion expresses a nostalgia for innocence and an appeal to the essence of being.
– Albert Camus, *The Rebel* (1951)

They were once 'communist bandits'. Now they are objects of nostalgia, national heroes to be rescued from history's neglect. For those who want to pay them homage the place to go is the 'peace villages' in Southern Thailand where ex-MCP guerrillas settled after the signing of the 1989 peace accord that formally ended the communist insurrection that began in 1948.[1] With a small university grant and the heart of one about to enter the lair of the beast, I went to seek them out.

Betong is some twenty minutes by car away from the Malaysian–Thai border checkpoint. It is a hot, grimy town; along the busy streets the shop signs announce the usual trades – souvenir shops, restaurants, leather goods, Thai massage, travel bureaus. Visitors come to shop and for the seafood, and not a few men for the sex. For some, though, the real attraction is Chulaporn Village No. 10 a few miles away. There are tour buses to the village, but to avoid the crowd I go out into the street and flag down a tut-tut scooter van. The driver is a young man with a dark greasy face who speaks some Mandarin, spitting out his words through the broken teeth. For an extra fifty baht, he will stop over at

---

1   See Agnes Khoo, *Life as the River Flows: Women and the Malayan anti-colonial struggle*, Petaling Jaya, Malaysia: SIRD, 2004, for an oral history account of the lives of ex-communist guerrillas settled in the Peace Villages.

the Winter Flower Garden, the hot spring and, as if he can read my ideological heart, the Piyamit Tunnel hideout of the Malayan communists. I take the bait.

The tunnel is of standing height, with packed-earth walls; a meandering path takes us to the underground office, the ammunition store and the meeting room. Inside the air is dense and humid. The visitors, with excited singing voices, snap away with their cameras. The young girls in shorts and slippers pose for selfies before the pile of Bren guns and rifles and rusty mines. In some parts the tunnel narrows and you have to pull in your shoulder as you turn. The place, with its thick airless dank and its clandestine past, stirs the mind. You try hard, and for a few moments you can just about call up the ghostly figure of a guerrilla-runner rushing from the headquarters to take the battle order to the front. You are supposed to be moved by the aura of the place, but I feel deflated and a bit foolish. Outside the sun and the dripping air beat upon us. We are vulnerable and chunky in our holiday clothes and don't know what to make of all this. It is a relief to get away.

Princess Chulaporn Village no. 10 sits in a lush valley. Silver streaks of the corrugated roofs break the expanse of tropical green as the land slopes gently up towards the distant hills. In mid-morning the mist clings to the forest still; but close to the road, the sun has sliced through the low clouds and shows up the rows of huts, neat and well-spaced like suburban dwellings; houses of the ex-guerrillas and their families. On the road people are walking about, each with a wide straw hat, one hand holding a basket, a scythe or a spade: a mundane village scene anywhere. The scooter taxi drops me off outside the History and Heritage Museum. Inside are the usual sad remains of the tools of the revolutionary – firearms, bullets, pamphlets and flags, aged and dust-covered on the display tables. Outside (the sign says: History Review – Betong Peace, Cultural and Tourist Village), I meet a group of young students. Chirpy as young birds, their faces wet from the heat and excitement, they have come from Singapore, a sprightly young woman tells me, to find out for themselves 'another history of the struggle for independence'. Putting down her video camera, she turns away and sets her sights on an old Chinese woman with a shopping basket walking by. She waves and calls out,

'Auntie, good morning, where you are going in such a hurry?'

'Oh, just to the shop to pick up a few things'.

The video camera is lodged back to the eye, to catch the woman's bouncy stride down the road. To her everything she sees is a photo opportunity and in her mind every stranger on the road is an ex-guerrilla fighter, an embodiment of revolution and anti-colonial struggle.

This was guerrilla tourism. If you think revolution, with its violence and clandestine conniving, is so full of gravity as to crush voyeuristic joy, think again. A couple of months ago I was in Yan'an, the old Red Army base in Xian, China, and I found myself among the mass of tourists inside the loess-earth caves that used to be the offices and sleeping-quarters of Mao and his colleagues. People snapped away with their digital cameras and smart phones at each other as they posed outside the caves. All that was missing here were *The East Is Red* in karaoke beat, women guides in brown khaki and cloth caps, and guerrilla packed lunches with Coke.

In the Peace Village the 'old comrades' ran shops and guesthouses and eating-places, and took tour groups to the old jungle camps and hideouts. I became tired of revolutionary relics, and one evening took myself to the Peace Restaurant. The restaurant offered the usual worker's fare – fried noodles, spicy pork (the menu said 'wild boar'), stir-fried sweet-potato leaves, swamp cabbage with shrimp sauce. Here, in the evenings the ex-guerrillas held court, and told tales of their endurance and great suffering in the jungle. I had arrived late, and sitting at the back I caught the jagged words through the crowd before me. 'Forget about the soldiers, the Gurkhas, we were not afraid of them. The most frightening were the bombers. They flew so high, just specks below the clouds. Then the bombs came: the explosions all around you, the horrible noise they made; you lay flat and tried to dig the ground with your fingers. . . .'

The storyteller tonight was Uncle Luo, the head-waiter. He knew the visitors had not come for the food, but for the stories of revolution that were still a political taboo south of the border in Malaysia and Singapore. Eager to pander to the audience, he also wanted to tell what he remembered of his revolutionary past. His eyes glistened, his voice a sad quiver as he spoke, stirred by what he had called up from memory. You felt he wanted us to know that he had not endured the struggle with the mute stoicism of beasts, that he had lived a life of mighty purpose and that nothing could be held against him.

A couple of nights later I caught up with Uncle Luo at the restaurant. Late in the evening there were only a sprinkle of customers – tuk-tuk drivers with their trademark neckerchiefs and sun-bleached singlets. The man before me at the other side of the table was in his seventies. He had tired, dusty eyes and his arms outside the shirtsleeves were wrinkled and brown; age and fatigue clung to every aspect of him. He sucked on his cigarette as he began to speak, lighting up his grave, ebony face. Born in a small settlement in Kajang near

Chin Peng, later General Secretary of the Malayan Communist Party and leader of the uprising, was among the MPAJA officers personally decorated by the British commander in chief, Lord Louis Mountbatten, in January 1946. (Source: photo still from film footage reproduced in the 1998 BBC documentary, 'Malaya - the Undeclared War', online at www.youtube.com/watch?v=pBRMRf0JVJc.)

Kuala Lumpur, he was a young eleven-year-old when the Japanese attacked and occupied Malaya. He couldn't remember much of the war years, but he could the exhilaration, the slide to unruly joy during the first months after the British return. The MCP-led Malayan People's Anti-Japanese Army (MPAJA) had fought a guerrilla war against the Japanese, and were, in the wartime alliance of convenience, British allies. Victory won, they were feted and disarmed in a ceremony at the *padang* opposite the government offices in Kuala Lumpur, and young Luo and his friends had gone to cheer the MPAJA heroes. They waved madly at one of the lorries and friendly hands hauled them up to join the communist fighters being conveyed to the parade. He recalls,

> We had only heard stories about these men, and here we were meeting them in the flesh. We were young and all stirred up. It was an exciting time. In the school, there were a lot of talks about how the communists were going to get organized, to make a better life for everyone. We all thought: the colonial masters would have different plans for the country, even allowing self-government. Now that the war's over, the communists would come out from the jungle and be allowed to do political work among the people.

A bamboo and palm shelter used as a kitchen at a recently abandoned communist insurgent camp located by Australian troops in Kedah state, February 1956. (Source: Australian War Memorial, P04683.004.)

Then he paused his elated tale, and said in a solemn voice: 'Well, you know how we were betrayed by the imperialists; they didn't keep their promises.'

Theirs was a revolutionary family. The two brothers and a sister all joined up. The elder Luo brother was secretary of the MCP Branch in Kajang, and his sister the organizer of the Kajang Youth and Women's Union Drama Society. When the Emergency started both were police targets. The Special Branch officers raided their house on a June night and arrested the elder brother who was later sentenced to repatriation to China. The two younger siblings escaped by seeking sanctuary with a band of MNLA (Malayan National Liberation Army) guerrillas in the jungle. The sister became a courier for the communist Min Yuen civil support team, while Luo himself, a youth of seventeen, joined his comrades in several ambushes and assassinations in towns and plantations in Kajang's Old River Port area. During a rainy night, he caught pneumonia while waiting at a jungle path for the target who never turned up. The pneumonia added to other ailments caused by living in the sunless jungle and by lack of food. In November 1951 the Party sent him to Hong Kong for treatment and recuperation, where he stayed four months. Of the three siblings only the sister was left in Malaya.

Luo was close to his sister. Their ages were only two years apart. He remembers how he and his mother used to wait late at night for his sister to make one of her clandestine visits. She always carried a bundle of pamphlets stuffed inside her blouse, other times it was a packet of medicine and an injection kit which he helped to bury under the banana tree at the back of the house. In the jungle both became combatants. Life consisted of intermittent episodes of rapid marches to lay ambushes and seek safety from security forces, followed by interludes of rest and the building of camp bases. At the camp, time was taken up with lectures, concerts and the cleaning of weapons. They read, studied and prepared the garden, before moving camp again. Years went by in a jumble of hazy recollections. He remembers the fatigue, the meals of boiled sweet potatoes and salted fish, the ulcer on his foot that rubbed against his rubber boots and made painful the jungle treks. Later, he was separated from his sister when she was sent away to lead a Min Yuen team in Perak. And he had to bear the news of his sister's 'martyrdom'. She was killed by a police patrol outside their house during one of her night visits to see their mother.

More than the dangers and sacrifices he endured, the killing of his sister affected him deeply. With her death, the abstract communist dialectics, the party's entreaty to armed struggle crumpled into the flaky banality of personal feelings. Luo paused to gather his thoughts. Outside the window the evening's last light was rapidly vanishing. Across the table, he lit another cigarette, and drawing in smoke he lifted his right hand found its way into his trouser pocket and took out his wallet. From the wallet a letter fell on the table before us, and he said faintly, 'Please take a look.' [2]

Dear Comrade Luo

Regarding your dear sister's martyrdom, please be informed that she was killed on 17 February, this year 1952, on Chulai Ninth Mile Road, betrayed by a despicable traitor. After the murder, her body was put on a parade in the street for all to see. This exposes the cruelty of the enemy and intensifies our hatred. She was a true revolutionary and respected by our leadership, and I hope this letter offers some consolation. Her martyrdom shows her sacrifice and her undying spirit. We remember this bloody debt and will take revenge on the running dogs.

Yu Min Kung
Liaison Committee
Selangor Branch
Communist Party of Malaya
12 April 1952

2   My translation of the original in Chinese. Document in possession of informant.

I checked my Sony digital recorder; we had been talking for more than an hour. I was deeply touched in spite of myself. It was a strange business; I was determined to shy away from the besieging crowd of guerrilla tourists, but found myself one of them. His stirring narrative had brought me to share a sense of his past. I was reminded of the communist apparatchik mother's bedroom in the film *Goodbye Lenin* (2003). She fell into a coma just before the unification of the two Germanys, and wakes up to a post-communist world while her mind is marooned in the past. Luo and I shared her 'Ostalgie' – nostalgia for the East – except for us the 'East' was the Red Malaya that never came about. The tetchiness that adhered to Luo like a dead insect on his skin testified to something – perhaps the oppressive sentimentality of his gloomy recollections, perhaps the way he embodied the romance of a failed revolution, with his loyalty still to the communist cause. I felt like telling him about the murderous doings of Stalin, Mao and Pol Pot, or more bookishly about the contradictions and the moral failures of the political ideology to which he had devoted his life. But that's historical hindsight, a great clarifier 'after the fact'. We are eager to make heroes of old revolutionaries who had carried our own hopes and innocence; while we were earth-bound in our petty needs and obsessions, they had broken free and joined the greatest adventure of modern times.

IN MALAYA THE COMMUNIST movement, led by the ethnic Chinese, came out of the struggle for modern China. Modern Chinese nationalism rose from the ashes of the Sino-British Opium War (1839–42).[3] China, which thought itself the centre of the civilized world, was defeated by 'barbarians' from across the sea who had come to enforce free trade. At the century's end, the disastrous six-month war with Japan in 1894–95 led to the annexation of Taiwan and southern Manchuria by the victor. For reformists like Kang Yuwei and Lian Qichao, China's serial defeats to foreign powers showed up more than its military weakness. To them China's cultural backwardness – all the antiquated ideas and Confucian rote-learning – was the real reason for the nation's impotence in the face of foreign incursions. Chinese culture and values had to be reformed and modernized.

The other cornerstone of Chinese cultural nationalism was the May Fourth Movement of 1919. Energized by the popular protest against Japanese expansion

---

3 For the broader domestic and international factors that led to the fall of the Qing Dynasty, a good guide is Frederic Wakeman, Jr. *The Fall of Imperial China*, New York: Free Press, 2007.

in China's northeast, May Fourth began with a series of student demonstrations demanding political reform and the boycotting of Japanese goods. Like the late Qing reformists, it also tied political change to a 'literary and cultural revolution'. May Fourth eventually morphed into a search for Chinese modernity, by calling for a radical evaluation of Chinese tradition and its values and the adoption of Western thoughts based on science and rational philosophy – Darwin, Spencer, Rousseau, Marx.

As a literary–intellectual movement, May Fourth harboured a deep conviction of the value of literature. Modern literature, accessible and using colloquial *pai hua* or plain speech, was to liberate the Chinese mind from – in Lu Xun's potent language in *The Madman's Diary* – the cannibalistic hold of tradition and mass subservience. China would be saved when its people were saved, and it was literature that would enlighten people with a new, modern cultural consciousness.[4]

In the South China Sea, Chinese migrants had little time for the 'cultural reforms' or 'modern literary aesthetics' of May Fourth. But they cared deeply about what happened in China. They had given support to Sun Yat-Sun's anti-Qing revolution and raised funds for it. Now they gathered force at a time when China was facing another crisis.

The second Sino-Japanese War (1937–45) began with the skirmishing between Japanese and Chinese troops that led to the Marco Polo Bridge incident, then quickly spread to the coastal cities and the central plain. Tientsin, Beijing, Shanghai and Nanking fell in 1937, Canton a year later. As news of devastation and the massacre of civilians reached Malaya, it prompted a fierce response. Malayan Chinese boycotted Japanese goods and organized relief for the war-torn homeland. Patriotism was a great leveller; in the anti-Japanese campaign, local organizers jostled with people of all shades – Guomindang supporters and communists, merchants and workers, teachers and students. The Sino-Japanese War was a significant training ground for the Malayan Chinese: it nurtured a new political consciousness, just as it taught them mass mobilization.

In the Peace Village the ex-guerrillas were wont to pepper their recollections with phrases like 'anti-imperialism', 'anti-colonial struggle' and 'socialist

---

4   Among the vast literature on Chinese modernity, I find most useful: Jonathan D. Spence, *The Gate of Heavenly Peace: The Chinese and their revolution, 1895–1980*, New York: Viking Penguin, 1981; Vera Schwarcz, Chinese Enlightenment, Berkeley: University of California Press, 1986; C.K. Wasserstrom and E.J. Perry (eds), *Popular Protest and Political Culture in Modern China*, Boulder, Colorado: Westview Press, 1994.

Malaya.' Becoming more abstract about culture and modernity would have spoilt their riveting tales. Yet there were plenty of abstractions in the struggle for modern China. Chinese modernity's faith in political change, its assault on the status quo, its elevation of 'scientific rationalism' over age-worn tradition: for many young Malayan Chinese it was often these rather than communism that first planted in them the seed of revolution. Chin Peng, the General Secretary of the MCP, remembered his early influences that gradually, fatefully, drew young people like him – he was 23 when he took up the top post of General Secretary in 1947 – towards the revolutionary path:

> After the Marco Polo bridge incident, Chinese journalists stationed in Ipoh came to my school. The school headmaster was quite patriotic – every Chinese at that time was patriotic – he was quite liberal in running the school. He was a graduate from an American-run university in the south of China, run by American Methodists ... [He called] a school meeting for all the students and then came this man Huang Shi ... Later on we came to know he was number two man in the Party ... He was the propaganda chief. We were very impressed by him. ... He analysed what happened in China, and the situation in China, and how we in Malaya [should support] China and we should get organised.[5]

This anti-Japanese resistance in China awakened in the young Chin Peng the force of political action in China which he now redirected to the struggle in Malaya.

> Conversion to communism is as strong as a religious conversion. It provided a faith and a belief in a system which, at least to the convert, appears as the incontrovertible path to what is right and fair among human beings. The depression years [of the thirties] and their aftermath, to our minds, provided ample proof that the inroads of colonialism and its associated capitalist political principles in South East Asia had to be thwarted. Our elders had watched as the British rounded up indentured Indian labour originally brought in to work the rubber plantations. Now unemployed and sleeping on the five-footways, the Indians, of no further use to their white masters, were promptly loaded onto freighters as deck cargo and deported back to their homeland. Things had to change.[6]

---

5   C.C. Chin and Karl Hack, *Dialogue with Chin Peng: New light on the Malayan Communist Party*, Singapore: Singapore University Press, 2004, pp. 57, 58–59.

6   Chin Peng and Ian Ward, *My Side of History*, Singapore: Media Masters, 2003, p. 47.

The MCP went through several metamorphoses before its formal founding in April 1930.[7] The Nayang General Labour Union (NGLU) formed in 1926 consisted of anarchists, labour organizers, Chinese Nationalists and communists, and came under the guidance of the Chinese Communist Party (CCP). After the collapse in 1927 of the CCP–Guomindang united front in China, the Malayan communists went their own way and formed the Malayan Revolutionary Committee (MRC) that fought both the Guomindang elements and the British. The MRC remained the key communist organization until the birth of the Nanyang Communist Party (NCP) in January 1928, the predecessor of the MCP.

In the first months of its birth, the NCP instigated a shoemakers' strike and some shoe shops were bombed. It undertook a massive propaganda drive, and produced pamphlets with rousing titles like 'Candle Light', 'Roaring Blast', 'Propertyless Youth', and 'Bolshevism'. To lend it multi-ethnic credentials, the NCP made efforts to recruit Malay followers; a communist named Ali was instructed to compose posters and leaflets in romanized Malay. It formed secret cells in schools where debates, lectures and dramatic performances helped to propagate modern, progressive ideas among young students; tactics the MCP was to later deploy with considerable success. The NCP was dissolved in April 1930 and the MCP took its place as the key communist organization in Malaya. The MCP came under the operational control of the Comintern's Far Eastern Bureau based in Shanghai, its agent the Vietnamese Nguyen Ai Quoc, the *nom de guerre* of Ho Chi Minh.

The position of the NCP had been a bewildering blend of anarchism, socialist utopianism, free speech and government of majority rule. As one leftist journal put it in 1919, '[H]uman character must be reformed into a new personality' in the building of a new society, and socialism was the 'criterion for reforming human character'.[8] Socialist revolution was to create new persons in a new era; it was to bridge the gulf between structural societal changes and the inner conversion of individuals. For all that, though, there was not yet talk of overthrowing British imperialism, or about how to foment a revolution in Malaya.

The early years of the MCP tell a story of state repression and police suspicion as it worked to build up a support base. The Malayan authorities were keen

---

7   An useful and concise early history of Malayan communism is: C.F. Yong, 'Origins and development of the Malayan Communist Movement, 1919–39', *Modern Asian History*, 25(4), 1991, pp. 625–648; see also by the same author, *The Origin of Malayan Communism*, Singapore: South Seas Society, 1997.

8   Yong, 'Origins and development of the Malayan Communist Movement, 1919–1939', p. 628.

to put a lid on industrial strikes and militant unionism, and to prevent the radical politics of China from spilling into the colony. The Communist–Guomindang wrangling had to be kept out of Malaya; and peace and order – and diplomatic appeasement of Japan – demanded that anti-Japanese demonstrations should not get out of hand. The 1930s were not a good time for the fledgling communist party. The MCP faced constant harassment, as the government imposed strict restrictions on its activities and imprisoned or deported many leading communists and labour organizers. Among the public there was yet to occur any widespread enthusiasm for national independence that could be translated into support for the MCP. The party had to wait for the great upheaval of a global war a decade later that would eventually define anti-colonialism, and anti-imperialism as popular causes.

The British return after the Second World War, for all the joyous sense of liberation and victory, was marked by chaos, lawlessness and administrative mess-ups. Not for nothing was the BMA, British Military Authorities, the caretaker government from September 1945 to May 1946, nicknamed 'Black Market Authorities'. Right until the outbreak of the Emergency in mid-1948, however, postwar Malaya had also witnessed political reform and cultural openness never before seen in the colony. The British authorities had set about repealing many of the restrictions on labour unions and political freedom, and the colonial society went through a flowering of political and cultural experiment, to which the writer Han Suyin gave the term 'Malayan Spring'.

The Malayan Spring came out of the new postwar political climate.[9] In the first general election after the war, the weary British public voted in a Labour government under Prime Minister Atlee with a plan for radical reform and the welfare state. But the colonies too were to enjoy a new sense of freedom, and development assistance was to be put in place to rehabilitate the social and economic life devastated by the war. In August 1947, the Singapore Social Welfare Conference brought together representatives of the South East Asian colonial governments and welfare groups to discuss how to give relief to local communities. The overall result of the reform, historian T. N. Harper writes warmly, was 'a widening of the public sphere, whereby new moods, vocabularies and techniques were introduced into political life that would resonate throughout the late colonial period'.[10]

---

9   See T.N. Harper, *The End of Empire and the Making of Malaya*, Cambridge: Cambridge University Press, 1999, pp. 75–92, for a brilliant scrutiny of the social, political and cultural effects of the Malayan Spring.

10 Ibid., p. 75.

The government liberal reform was an experiment in forging a 'new conception of empire'.[11] For the Malayan people, the experience was intermittently one of official largesse and relaxation of rule followed by restriction and censure. Much was at stake for the colonial authorities. In the shaping of the colonial society, they would ensure that the openness and liberalization were to be defined in terms of political expediency and the imperial interest. During the Second World War Britain had desperately needed the colonies' manpower and resources. Social and economic development – and the talk of independence or at least self-government – had helped to appease the nationalists and to recruit support for Britain's war effort. When the war ended, the prospect of chaos and shortages in the colonies made Britain re-examine its earlier policies. The new approach was to rebuild the colonial society, but as one that would cooperate with the authorities and help in restoring social order and imperial legitimacy.

In the euphoric atmosphere, in December 1945, the MCP signed an agreement with the government to disband the MPAJA. The Party, too, was responding to the fresh liberal climate. It believed it could gain power through united front politics and through open elections. Through its front organization, the Ex-Comrades Association, the MCP began to spread its influence and build a network of alliances under the banner of progressive liberalism and socialism. For the MCP anything seemed achievable. And it could well afford the illusion, for social conditions – and history itself – were at last in the communists' favour, or so it appeared.

SHE ASKS ME NOT to use her name, but gets me to call her Xiao Hong, her *nom de guerre* of the guerrilla days. Perhaps she should thank the Malaysian government; luckier than some of her comrades, after the 1989 peace accord she was granted permission to return and live with her kin in Malaysia. In the small pleasant room of a terrace house in Kepong, near Kuala Lumpur, she talks to me with a plucky self-revelation that unsettles my academic leftism. For before me is a revolutionary in the flesh. She is a woman of a bygone era, yet her sparkling eyes, her profile, preserve some of the carefreeness of her younger self. Settled in a cane chair next to the morning window, she is like an old classmate you meet at a high school reunion. Her now wrinkled face, along with that demure smile, conceals another identity, another time that you have no inkling of. Her fellow comrade Uncle Luo at the peace village exuded no avuncular warmth and openness; his words were mostly stiff sloganeering.

---

11 Ibid.

Here, though, is someone who is rich with an inner life and who has a strong sense of herself.

Her journey to revolution took the familiar route: the political education while in the communist cell in high school; the harassment and threat of arrest by the police; the Party's order to join the comrades in the jungle. But her heart is not in it when she tells me these things, and I have been too long in the research game not to catch the polite hesitancy of an informant.

For a while we nurse our cups of green tea, then she reaches into the under pocket of her dark-blue blouse and takes out a photograph. 'It's a picture of me. I must have been seventeen or eighteen then, quite a looker, don't you think?', she says as her crinkled face breaks into a smile. I take the picture in my hand. She is standing on a beach underneath a coconut palm, the wind pressing on her dress and beneath, the flesh of a young body – an appearance of unfussy robustness and health under the tropical sun. Her face is petite, expressive, and the bobs of dark hair that gently curl down to graze at the chin emitted no air of vanity. 'It was the style of the time. The Hong Kong film stars all had this kind of cut in those days.'

She was a seamstress then, around 1953, living in a rented room on top of one of the shophouses in Petaling Street in Kuala Lumpur's Chinatown. Each room was divided by wooden boards, with a low iron bed pushed against the wall on each side. It was close-quarters living, like aspiring actors in a budget boarding house waiting for the big break. The other tenants were like her, young working women seeking a direction in life, each aspiring to something 'serious' though they didn't know what it was. Like her friends, she was fond of reading – novels, translations of Western classics, film magazines, local progressive newspapers. Her lack of English alienated her from Anglo-American culture. But there were pop songs and films from Hong Kong. Offerings of the leftist Great Wall Studio were a great attraction. The studio is 'patriotic' directors turned their hands to realistic treatments of life in an office or a factory in the capitalist British colony. Each tale was spiced up with the 'political soul searching' of a young worker – always a woman and played by one of Great Wall's glamorous stars – as she turns her experience of injustice into self-discovery. Besides consciousness-raising films, Great Wall had its stock of celebrities. When the beautiful, feisty Xia Meng – the voluptuous Gong Li of the time but one with an ideological attitude – came to town, Xiao Hong had taken leave and joined the enamoured fans at the airport and returned triumphantly with the star's autograph. At home, lingering in the excitement, she had put on a record of Xia Meng and listened in an adoring daze to the perky melody about a love-forlorn rickshaw driver luckless in love and too poor to find a wife ...

In the fifties, the Emergency laws had put a lid on most forms of political expression. Nevertheless, public demonstrations and labour protests took place openly with or without a police permit; and there were simply too many leftist books and newspaper articles propounding 'progressive views' for the authorities to keep track of. Xiao Hong was not yet a 'flag-waving radical', but she, who had finished three years in Kuen Cheng Girls' Chinese High School in Kuala Lumpur, remembers the student unrest over the many government plans to rein in the Chinese schools and the radical students. In May 1954 some of her school friends went down to Singapore to lend support to a demonstration against the introduction of national service. She resisted joining them; she had yet to make up her mind about such things. Remembering her parents in the village, she was not so reckless as to get into trouble with the authorities. Her political coming of age was unhurried; instant conversion was not her way. In any case, she was not exactly unoccupied. She travelled each day to the small factory where, with ten other seamstresses, she turned out cotton pyjamas, men's underwear, blouses, and boys' shorts. Once a month, she picked a day and visited her parents; she went to the pictures and she took Sunday outings to the Lake Gardens with friends where they talked about life and work and love's triumphs and betrayals. And she read.

It is a particular character of the time that a young, educated person like Xiao Hong should have had available to her a literary culture both dazzlingly modern and cosmopolitan. In Malaya the Chinese-language schools and the government English schools sat on a ridge of class divide. The English schools, whose names – Victoria Institution, Methodist Boys' School, Bukit Nanas Convent School – told of their colonial and missionary origins, attracted children from the professional and the Anglo-Malayan elite. The Chinese schools had a more frugal and modest foundation. Funded by the Chinese community and philanthropists, they taught a curriculum of modern learning and a mixture of contemporary literature and traditional Chinese classics. Children of small shopkeepers, hawkers and labourers went to the Chinese schools. Limited means and the lack of English put them there, while some parents saw these school as offering the best education for their children as a way of keeping in touch with the culture of the ancestral land. The English schools socialized you into the world of Connie Francis and Elvis Presley, Sunday School, the novels of John Buchan, John Blackmore and Robert Louis Stevenson in the Longman Simplified English series. The Chinese schools gave their students a medley of cultural nationalism, Chinese identity and a sense of life's grave purposes. The teachers – the most dedicated were exiles from the Japanese invasion and the civil war in China – set about drilling into young minds in the virtues of 'modern education' and progressive ideas. Unburdened by the longing for things 'British', students made a bid for something more cosmopolitan. For some, they were to 'find themselves', as we say these days, through the polemics and the unalloyed pleasures of Chinese literary texts and modern Western classics – Gogol, Turgenev, Jack London, Ibsen, Zola – that came out of the Foreign Languages Press of Beijing and were sold in the local bookshops. For young students like Xiao Hong the modernist struggle in the work of Ba Jin, whose *Family, Spring, Autumn Trilogy* was an eloquent eulogy of the search for personal freedom that came out of May Fourth, found a powerful affirmation in *Madam Bovary*. Both cry out, through their protagonists, for a life that longs 'to make music that will melt the stars'.

How wonderful it is to think that a young Malayan Chinese woman, a simple seamstress, was moved to tears by Chekov or Flaubert rendered into the Chinese language. It was a time when everyday culture delivered a hodgepodge of modern values and yearnings. The Great Wall Studio films were enjoyable and slyly instructive, as were the newspapers. In the leisure hours after dinner, she told me, she would pore over a copy of the *China Press* or the *Nanyang Siang Pao*, picking through the headline news, the movie star gossip, the 'women's column' of health advice and new recipes, and finishing up with the supplement.

The supplement – *fuzhang* – was one or more pages inserted in the main part, dealing with light, practical issues. It offered business advice, tips on personal grooming, travel notes, film reviews; and it included a literary forum which published essays, poems and short stories written sometimes by in-house writers but more often sent in by readers and professional writers. Xiao Hong could do without the business tips and health advice, but the literary forum captivated her. These writings were full of distinctive, leftist themes about the workers' plight, and public protests over harsh government actions of one form or the other. Often the essays, short stories and poems took a critical stance against both Chinese tradition and colonial society itself. It is easy to picture her knitting her brow and being moved by issues concerning socialist struggle and revolution cast in veiled words and metaphors. She was not one to boast about her learning or her modern ideas; to get a sense of these 'progressive newspapers' I went to the National University of Singapore library to read first hand the Malayan Chinese leftist literature and find out what were in the 'supplements'.

In the dusty hold of the university archive, 'patriotism', 'new cultural movement', 'enlightenment', and 'freedom' leapt from the pages like sleeping insects disturbed. This fair example appeared in the *fuzhang* pages in one of the newspapers on 13th May 1954.

May

May, the piteous May.
The hot breath blowing across the land
Makes me remember the 'May Fourth' of another time.
Why did people stand up to the guns?
Why did people fill the prisons?
They are the sparks of the Chinese race –
the eternal brilliance of our race!

May, the piteous May.
Windless, it will not unsettle and disturb.
This is the ancient wisdom of the Great Wall
This is the revival of the Chinese national spirit.

May, the piteous May.
The sun of midsummer makes for a miserable life
My dear one:
In the dark recess against the wall
Let us talk about our own story of May.[12]

Typical of the leftist Malayan-Chinese writing of the time, *May* is full of naïve lyricism and nationalist longing, with barely disguised references to the other May event in China, the 1919 May Fourth Movement. There were plenty of other such calls in the newspapers: Chinese modernity was the inspiration for the struggle in the colony.[13]

Socialist realism also made its appearance in the literature of the time. In this poem, the use of a Malay word (*tolong* is the Malay for 'help' or 'mercy') was a localizing sign that shifts the polemics to the dire conditions in colonial Malaya.

---

12 *Nanyang Siang Pao*, 13 May 1955, p. 5.
13 For the influence of the May Fourth Movement in Malaya, see David L. Kenley, *New Culture in a New World: the May Fourth Movement in Singapore, 1919–1932*, New York: Rouledge, 2003.

Cry not 'Tolong!'

All those jobless and without hope
Crying 'tolong!'
All those weak with hunger
Crying 'tolong!'
It is a word of the man-eat-man, exploitative society!

All that is left between man and man is the cry of 'tolong'.
Let us arise and do battle with 'tolong'.
In a new society, no one shall cry 'tolong'.
In the day of freedom and equality, no one shall cry 'tolong'.
You'll see, the day will come!
There will be no more cries of 'tolong' among the people.[14]

If the young Xiao Hong had found in the poem much of calling for blood and confrontation, there was no shortage of writings with a feminist thrust. It is nice to think of her chancing upon *Girls in White Skirts*, and being touched by the blend of message-bearing and ethnographic realism.

Girls in White Skirts[15]

The girls are dancing, the girls are singing.
This one is running, that one is leaping.
Bodies as agile as eagles.
The girls with long pleated hair.

The red smiling faces.
Like a red ripe apple.
In the hearts flow hot blood
of justice, passion and unrivalled strength.

The blood on your feet stains the mud and sand you walk on.
Sending consoling words to the miserable farmer.
Your bold cries pierce the cloud
and touch the wounded souls.

14 Cheah See Kian, *Malayan Chinese Left Wing Literature: Its influence by China (sic) Revolutionary Literature (1926–1976)*, Penang, Malaysia: Han Chiang College, 2009, pp. 151–152; my translation.

15 Cheah, *Malayan Chinese Left Wing Literature*, pp. 160–161; my translation.

On the stage of candlelight.
In the voices that behold the glory of our culture and race.
Among the people thirsting for hope.
The girls in white skirts, how glorious you are.
You say that a comfortable life puts a chain on progressive ideas.
Glorious learning comes from the people,
their pain, their misfortune, their sickness, their death.
You will sweep these sufferings from the world.

Your have thrust your bodies to the furnace.
Bravely endured the heat and the refining fire.
You say that fish cannot separate from water, a person cannot leave
    the people.
We march forward, and break the cage of individualism.
You walk the glorious path of martyrs.
In the tropics the bright sun and evening stars.
are like the torch of liberty and happiness –
reflections in your eyes.

Here also is the code for socialism and the cry for political change, in which Mao's 'fish and water' metaphor for guerrilla tactics makes a sly appearance. The argument for a new position for women is made, but the call for revolutionary violence is unmistakable – all the bloody feet and red-stained sand and mud. Putting the body to the furnace avers to the refinement of personal commitment in the fire of revolutionary action, an echo of Nikolay Ostrovsky's 1932 novel *How the Steel Was Tempered*, regarded by intellectuals in China and Malaya as the iconic novel of socialist realism.

In the editor's fastidious selections, the poems and essays that found their way to the supplements and anthologies were politically rather than emotionally gripping. Typical of the socialist realist mode, the central figures were simple working people and when love raised its head the longing and vicissitudes were cast on the figure of a labourer, a factory worker, a rickshaw driver. A rickshaw driver, lonely and wifeless, was a plot that appeared in not a few short stories. It's a cliché, yet his lucklessness and lack of means tell of the social injustices facing one such as he: the tradition of 'bride price' needed to acquire a wife; the drudgery and poor return of his work. And at the forefront, like a steam engine lugging the loaded carriages, is the certainty of change, the inevitability of social betterment for all.

All this – modern Chinese literary texts, the translated works of Western modern classics, the Great Wall Studio films, the poems and essays and short stories of the newspaper 'literary supplement' – made for the influences that shaped Xiao Hong's life. What one eventually becomes is mysterious, determined by things both unexpected and complex. In any case, for Xiao Hong it was a remarkable transformation from a young seamstress to a communist revolutionary, a transformation aided by the unlikely kinship of Ba Jin, Flaubert, Sinclair Lewis and Soviet socialist realism. But that may be slightly over-simplifying.

The doctor–writer Han Suyin, who practised medicine in Malaya throughout the fifties, was sure of communism's importance to the struggles of Asia. She writes:

> To divide the world into communist and anti-communist faiths is to obscure realities, not to explain the monstrous necessity which drives men into action. The differences are in speed and method toward a common aim: food, shelter, social security, a living wage, social justice, education ... In Asia today whichever country or nation is going to achieve this basic social security within the next twenty years for the greatest number of its people, is likely to set the pattern for others.[16]

MANY SAW COMMUNISM AS offering the best, speediest solution to the problems of food and shelter. However, progressives like Han Suyin were also fervent modernists. They talked of a 'rice bowl' revolution in Asia, but they were not blind to the culture and tradition that mired people in social and economic backwardness, that sapped their will for direct political action. The echoes of May Fourth were clear and distinct. Communism was the lucid expression of the unity of social–cultural and economic struggles. For the authors of *The Communist Manifesto* the crux of revolutionary progress is modernity; the dynamic, whirling changes of the world and the feelings and impulses they stir up. Chinese writers and intellectuals took to this idea with all the zealousness of the newly converted, for here was something that promised to do away with the traditionalism, the mental subservience they saw as the Chinese obstacle to a new world. For young women like Xiao Hong the struggle for food and shelter was one thing. But she was no crude materialist. Communism, fed to her mind through a perplexing range of texts and influences, was also irresist-

---

16 Han Suyin, 'Social change in Asia', *Suloh Nantah: Journal of the English Society, Nanyang University*, Singapore, 15–16, 1960, p. 2.

ible for the optimism and personal discovery that both Marxism and Flaubert's *Madame Bovary*, in their different ways, offered.

I get up from my chair and say goodbye, and she, leaning herself on the arm of the Indonesian maid, walks me to the door. At the gate facing the sun-drenched road, for a while I don't know what to say. I hear her polite words thanking me for coming to see her, and in my heart I feel foolishly, uncontrollably, sentimental towards the old woman who has lived a life whose magic and sacrifice I can barely comprehend. She has let free her thoughts and they have touched mine, a miracle of connection that occasionally blesses the researcher. Her reminiscences have hooked me up to my student days when the war in Vietnam and the anti-colonial struggles still had the innocence of political hope, their violence and bloodshed redeemable by the rightness of their causes. But now the fall of the Berlin Wall, and the moral venality of communist regimes had changed everything. And in that afternoon in her room we have been united by our own irrelevance. I look at her as her eyes turn to a soft glistening. To cover the embarrassment I do all the talking. I say I'll come back to see her and I hope that her health will hold up for years to come. She looks tired and yet exudes a certain dignity of one who has lived through and done great things. She has taken part in a great adventure, and the romantic aura of this will never leave her.

3 On Violence
Imperial policing and British counter-insurgency

[T]he power and resolution of the Government forces must be displayed. Anything which can be interpreted as weakness encourages those who are sitting on the fence to keep on good terms with the rebels.
– Major-General Sir Charles W. Gwynn, *Imperial Policing* (1934)

Power is neither exercised nor witnessed without emotion.
– A.P. Thorton, *The Imperial Idea and Its Enemies: A study of British power* (1959)

The first shots of the Malayan Emergency were fired at 8.30am on June 16, 1948, in the office of the Elphil Estate twenty miles east of the Sungei Siput town, Perak. Arthur Walker, the 50-year-old manager, after making the rounds of the rubber plantation, had just returned to the office for some paper work. After breakfast he had said goodbye to his wife who was driving into town to do some shopping in preparation for the voyage to England for home leave. A few minutes before 8.30am three young Chinese men rode up to the office on bicycles. They leaned the bicycles against the building and walked casually up the steps to the door. The dog barked as they entered the office and Walker tried to calm it. One of the men said to him, in Malay, 'Greetings, Sir!' Walker returned the greeting, then two shots rang out. The Indian clerk in the next room rushed into Walker's office. His boss's body lay by the office safe, shot through the heart. The contents of the safe were untouched; they had not come for the money.

Half an hour later, ten miles away, twelve armed men surrounded the main building of the Phin Soon Estate. John Allison, the 55-year-old manager was in the office, and in the adjacent room his young assistant, Ian Christian. The

MNLA men entered the office and marched the Europeans at gunpoint to a nearby bungalow. Allison had told them his revolver was there. Having secured the revolver, they took the two men back to the office. 'Don't be afraid,' one of the gunmen assured the frightened clerks. 'We are only out for the Europeans and the running dogs.' They bound and tied Allison and Christian to the chairs and shot them. The planned execution was to include a third Briton in an estate a few miles out of Sungei Siput. But his jeep had broken down during the morning inspection and he was late in returning to the office. Another group of gunmen had been sent out to kill him; they could not wait and left. Two days later, on June 18, 1948, the British authorities declared a countrywide state of Emergency. The Malayan Emergency war had begun.

This, on the start of the Emergency as recounted in Noel Barber's *The War of The Running Dogs*,[1] is a classic victor's narrative. The book, widely read and quoted, has over the years come to serve as the popular British version of the conflict. For here is the adroit telling of a counter-insurgency in a distant colony, a story peopled with cunning police and special branch officers who knew a thing or two about fighting a dirty war; doughty planters who defiantly did their rounds of golf and pink gins at the club by arriving in armour-plated cars; and of course, the plucky memsahibs, Bren gun against the shoulder, helping to repulse a communist night assault that came straight out of the film *The Planter's Wife* (1952). A seasoned reporter with years in the East, Barber knew how to tell a riveting tale. As war stories go, though, the Sungei Siput assassination was neither raw nor gory. All in all, three people were killed but it sparked off a full-scale war in which, at its height in 1952, some 40,000 British and Commonwealth troops, 67,000 police and 250,000 Home Guards were pitted against 7,200 insurgents, resulting in nearly 3,000 civilian casualties.[2] But that, you feel, is not the important thing. The authorial trick is to give British actions unignorable reasonableness and heroism, while the communists appear only in police mug shots or as withered corpses by the jungle path after an ambush. Barber is too sharp a writer to go for hack phrases. Yet he might as well have settled for 'senseless killing' and 'clumsy stupidity' when describing the actions of insurgents. We remember the insurgents' cool-headed dispatching of the planters tied and gagged, while missing out the third target, and while Walker was murdered, they missed out his wife out shopping. (Did the MNLA men

---

1   Noel Barber, *The War of The Running Dogs*, London: Fontana, 1971.

2   Karl Hack, 'The Malayan Emergency as counter-insurgency paradigm', *Journal of Strategic Studies*, 32(3), 2009, p.414.

really intend to kill the British woman?) 'Senseless killing' has just enough of the Cold War demonization of communists to depict an enemy driven by brutality and sadistic thrill. Theirs is not the side of God and civilization.

Yet for the insurgents Sungei Siput was far from being an operation of random killing. It was carried out against the backdrop of labour unrest over wage cuts by the estates at a time of declining rubber prices. A year earlier in November Chinese labourers had gone on strike over the issue, and rumours were circulating that Walker and Allison had mistreated their workers and con-nived with the police to break the strike.[3] Sungei Siput lies in the Kinta Valley, a region of tin mines and rubber estates. At the region's jungle fringes were farmers squatting on government land since the Japanese occupation, trying to hack out a living in the wilderness. The labour conditions and the squatter-farmers had created the classic 'revolutionary situation' which the MCP were quick to exploit. For the communists, the Sungei Siput killings were far from random or senseless. Just as decades later in Vietnam tax collectors and Saigon-appointed village chiefs were singled out by the Viet Cong for elimination, European planters as a symbol of British colonialism made meaningful targets of revolutionary violence. The killings showed the daring of the communists, just as they generated fear among those keen to do the government's bidding.

That matters little, however. For Barber's telling of the Emergency typifies the understanding by the average Malaysian of the violent episode in their national history. Not only Sungei Siput but the whole communist uprising was without social and moral reasoning. Violence and brutality were the sole preserve of the insurgents. On the other hand, in a narrative like this, govern-ment repression is always handled with a great deal of soft-gloved shrewdness. To justify Britain's counter-insurgency measures in Malaya, it is enough to call up the values that defined the nature of colonial rule: liberalism, humanitari-anism and civilized conduct. In the Emergency, these values were to provide the 'moral template' of government policies, and how British troops should conduct themselves.

WHEN THE EMERGENCY WAS declared the government found itself in a state of confusion. The MCP's turn to armed insurrection caught everyone by sur-prise. In 1945 when the Second World War ended, the Malayan communists, who had fought against the Japanese, enjoyed an uneasy peace with the Brit-ish authorities. The party devoted itself to united front politics, building up

---

3   T.N. Harper, *The End of Empire and the Making of Malaya*, pp. 113–114.

influence in the labour unions, trade associations and student organizations. In the openness of the immediate postwar period, it believed it had a role in the reconstruction of Malaya by gaining political power and harnessing its reputation as a force of anti-Japanese resistance. Towards the end of 1947, a change of the MCP leadership and the increasing British repression – including, most notoriously, banishment of 'criminals and subversives' to China – prompted the MCP to take up arms. In early 1948 the party leadership instigated a wave of strikes and labour unrest throughout Malaya, inviting further government repression. The Sungei Siput killings were the culmination of the MCP change of strategy.

As it turned out, the government had little inkling of the new MCP strategy; 'the intelligence apparatus was in a woeful state', and the Malayan Security Service (MSS) had failed to give unequivocal warning.[4] In a way the Emergency was forced on the British by the killing of the three planters. In the early months, chaos and lack of direction immobilized the government. On the military front, the security forces did not know how to fight an enemy moving freely in the jungle and enjoying support from the Chinese rural population. British planters and miners, who bore the brunt of the communist attacks, began to talk about government incompetence and being betrayed by Whitehall.

Historians and strategic studies experts have marked out 1948–51 as an exceptional period of the Emergency. They are candid about the practices of 'counter-terror' by the government and its security forces. Violence and repression all but defined the approach to counter-insurgency.[5]

British forces including Commonwealth troops – reaching 40,000 at the opening of the 1950s – assisted by police were deployed to tighten the grip on the countryside. Senior officers veered between over-optimism and ineptness; General Ritchie, the commander British forces, thought the communists would be pushed out of the settled areas by the end of 1948.[6] Many believed large-scale military offensives would work, and putting pressure on the villagers would bring them over to the government's side. By September, however,

---

4   Huw Bennett, '"A very salutary effect": The counter-terror strategy in the early Malayan Emergency, June 1948 to December 1949', *Journal of Strategic Studies*, 32(3), 2009, p. 420; Karl Hack, 'British intelligence and counter-insurgency in the era of decolonization. The example of Malaya', *Intelligence and National Security*, 14(2), 1999, pp. 99–125.

5   Huw Bennett outlines the government counter-terror strategy in 'A very salutary effect'.

6   Ibid., p. 424.

The body of a communist insurgent, shot after being tracked for three days by Australian soldiers, 1956–58. (Source: Australian War Memorial, P09312.002.)

three months into the Emergency, the Far East Land Forces (FARELF) were voicing a note of caution: 'It is becoming noticeable that during the period of Military activity the flow of information improves and Gangster acts decrease, but that after Military Operations are completed the reverse process occurs.'[7]

In this situation many in the government began to push for a hard line. Air Marshal Sir Hugh Lloyd, commander of air forces in the Far East theatre, believed in gain from punishing the population: 'Perhaps the best encouragement for people to give information would be to hang some of the enemies.' Malcolm MacDonald, the Commissioner-General, thought more or less along the same lines; he was certain that 'show of force would be helpful' and that the Chinese should be handled 'with great firmness'.[8]

However, 'firmness' was one thing, another the actual fighting which involved a lot of 'jungle bashing' – frustrating and yielding little. The British forces launched large sweeps through the jungle, hundreds or thousands of soldiers fanning out on a broad front, trekking through the bush like parties of partridge shooters. They were noisy and visible affairs. Though there were no children selling Coke and cigarettes as was the case with American patrols in Vietnam, news of amassing troops quickly travelled through the MNLA grapevine. The element of surprise was lost. The guerrillas invariably chose to

---

7   Ibid., p. 424.

8   Ibid., pp. 427–8.

Detail from an exposé, published in the British *Daily Worker* on 10 May 1952, of widespread killings in Malaya by the British. These revelations were dismissed as communist propaganda and largely ignored by the British public. (Courtesy: IpohWorld, www.ipohworld.org.)

avoid battle and melted away through jungle trails. With elusive enemies and inhospitable jungle terrain, the British forces found it near impossible to locate the insurgents and close in for the kill. A major in a British rifle company remarked: 'The bigger operations . . . and higher the level at which it was planned, the less its chance of success; the buildup and the preparation were impossible to conceal . . . the guerrillas simply vanished.' In the chaos and frustration, he warned, 'it was difficult to control troops in the jungle.'[9]

---

9   Raffi Gregorian, '"Jungle Bashing" in Malaya: Towards a formal Tactical Doctrine', *Small Wars and Insurgencies*, 5(3), 1994, p. 341.

'Jungle bashing' was not without some success, though. The MNLA still tended to be over-confident and underestimate the strength of the government forces, which increasingly deployed air power to locate and destroy the insurgent camps. Tight censorship was still in place, and the successes of the security forces were widely reported. After an ambush, as a warning to the public, the bodies of the communist dead were dumped outside the police station or laid out in the town square. Government troops severed the heads of guerrillas killed and brought them back for identification. This only came to public knowledge when, in May 1952, the British Communist Party paper *The Daily Worker* printed a photo of a Royal Marine Commando posing gleefully with the heads of two insurgents, a man and a woman.

The period also saw significant numbers of persons shot 'while attempting to escape'. In one of the earliest incidents, on 21 July 1948, the police in response to an attack on the Elphil Estate in Perak state, 'shot two Chinese who refused to stop when called upon to do so'. On 8 August, in Bentong, Pahang state, a Chinese man was shot 'while trying to escape after arrest'. Historian Huw Bennett, who quotes these incidents, comments laconically, 'Here, as elsewhere, there can be no certainty about whether these people were truly shot trying to escape, or if it was a euphemism for murder.'[10] In November, during Operation Rugger, an army-police search resulted in 102 arrests, of whom 39 were identified as 'bandits' and detained; eleven were killed while attempting to escape.[11]

The most notorious incident took place in Batang Kali, a Chinese village of rubber tappers and tin-mine workers in Selangor state on 12 December 1948. A fourteen-man patrol of the 2nd Battalion of the Scots Guards arrived and put the villagers through a hard grilling. They wanted to know the whereabouts of the communists and accused the villagers of aiding and giving food to the 'bandits'. The men and women were then separated. A woman was crying and the soldiers threatened to shoot her if she didn't stop. The womenfolk and their children spent the night in a room without food or water. The next morning as they were being put into a lorry, they saw the men tied up and being taken away; a few minutes later they heard a series of shots. As the lorry was pulling away, the soldiers torched the houses, destroying everything inside. Twenty-four men were killed; one feigned death and survived. The official statement was that they had been shot while trying to make a mass escape into the jungle.

---

10 See Huw Bennett, 'A very salutary effect', p. 434.

11 Ibid.

The Scots Guards had been well deployed, and the 'bandits' had run into their line of fire. In the 1970 British investigation, the soldiers interviewed kept to the 'shooting while the men were attempting to escape' explanation, and maintained that an order had been given to them to open fire. One soldier of the Scots Guards platoon remembered that a sergeant had said beforehand, 'The villagers are going to be shot.' Another recalled:

> There was an inquiry later on and I've got to go along with this, we were told before going in to tell the same story, that is that the bandits were running away when they were shot . . . I don't remember who told us to tell this story but it was a member of the army.'[12]

Several official enquires were held. The original investigation of December 1948, conducted by the Malayan Attorney-General, Sir Stafford Foster Sutton, did not call survivors as witnesses, or carry out forensic examinations. It exonerated the soldiers. The Batang Kali massacre re-emerged in the public eye more than half a century later, in May 2012, when the relatives of the dead sought redress by bringing the case before the British High Court. The judges ruled that the appellants' case 'contradicts claims made by successive British governments', the *Guardian* newspaper reported, and dismissed an attempt by the victims' families to set up a public inquiry into the event'. No soldiers were charged.[13]

The *Guardian* newspaper also revealed that after the killings, 'The British authorities hastily passed a regulation empowering troops in the country to use "lethal force" to prevent escape attempts.' Regulation 27A was unveiled on 20 January 1949 by Sir Alec Newboult, chief secretary of the Federation of Malaya, little more than a month after the Batang Kali massacre. Newboult's command authorized 'the use of lethal weapons' to 'prevent the escape from arrest, so long as a warning was first issued'.[14] Tellingly, Regulation 27A carried retrospective power, such that any 'act or thing done before the coming into force of this regulation' would be immune from prosecution.

---

12 'Batang Kali massacre: British soldiers admitted unlawful killings, court told', *The Guardian*, 9 May 2012. The massacre is mentioned in practically all historical accounts of the Emergency, casting different degrees of moral culpability on the British forces.

13 *The Guardian*, 21 March 2014.

14 'Revealed: how Britain tried to legitimise Batang Kali massacre', *The Guardian*, 6 May 2012.

The alleged massacre took place more than half a century ago in a colonial war. What makes it newsworthy is the way the British army conducted itself, and more so the continuing denial and whitewashing by the past and present governments. The issue surely is not whether Batang Kali would open the floodgates for compensation claims if the UK government admitted culpability. For by 2013 it had already agreed to pay limited compensation to victims of the Kenya Emergency.[15] But Malaya is not Kenya. In the public imagination, the conflict in the Malayan jungle was an honest anti-communist undertaking where British values and traditional decency had been, for the most part, strictly observed.

In many ways, the troops of the Scots Guards cannot be said to have been operating without 'rules of engagement' when they turned on the Batang Kali villagers. Even if the British high command did not order the killing, the soldiers would have taken to heart the febrile atmosphere at the time, just as they would have government pronouncements such as this by the High Commissioner Sir Henry Gurney:

> [T]errorists can be defeated only by the initiative being taken by the Police and other security forces against the terrorists on their own ground and according to their own rules. . . . It is in fact impossible to maintain the rule of law and to fight terrorism effectively at the same time. I have publicly said that it is paradoxical though none the less true that in order to maintain law and order in present conditions in Malaya it is necessary for the Government itself to break it for a time. . . . At the present time the Police and Army are breaking the law everyday.

He then set out to absolve government forces from the consequences of acting outside the law:

> [I]t is most important that police and soldiers, who are not saints, should not get the impression that every small mistake is going to be the subject of a public enquiry or that it is better to do nothing at all than to do the wrong thing quickly. . . . [Government measures] can only be permanently successful if some alternative affiliation, stronger than the bandits and at the same time inspiring greater fear, can be introduced to which the floating Chinese can attach themselves.[16]

---

15 In 2003 the British government agreed to pay £2,600 each to 5,000 survivors of government camps in colonial Kenya; see 'Kenya: UK expresses regret over abuse as Mau Mau promised payout', *The Guardian*, 6 June 2013.

16 See Huw Bennett, 'A very salutary effect', p. 432.

The British policy carefully avoided calling the conflict a war. Captured insurgents were thus treated as common criminals rather than prisoners of war protected by the Geneva Convention. (Source: photo still from film footage reproduced in the 1998 BBC documentary, 'Malaya - the Undeclared War', online at www.youtube.com/watch?v=pBRMRf0JVJc.)

For the individual trooper such pronouncements no doubt gave licence to a certain behaviour. But he must have also believed that he belonged to a modern army that fought on the side of democracy and was not given to massacre civilians and prisoners of war. Barely three years ago they and their US – and Russian – allies had fought in the grand crusade against Axis tyranny in Europe and Asia; now the fight against communism was again a fight for decency and civilization.

For us, it is a taxing issue how to reconcile a military misdeed like Batang Kali with the British military ethos as we know it. For some the solution lies in the familiar route of 'exceptionalism'. For the government and some in academic circles Batang Kali was an 'exception', an unfortunate 'indiscretion' and 'misdemeanour'. Anthony Short, for instance, was certain that the soldiers were operating within the law, that 'people were not shot out of hand as a matter of policy', and that such instances were 'the exception';[17] though he has since changed his mind after the *Guardian* revelations.

---

17 Anthony Short, *The Communist Insurrection in Malaya 1948–1960*, London: Frederick Muller, 1975, p. 160.

'Exceptionalism' is a well-oiled means of vindication for Western powers' misconduct in counter-insurgencies (compare: My Lai, Abu Ghraib, Northern Ireland). It settles the idea that the killing of civilians is not what Western armed forces normally do on the battlefield. Like 'collateral damage', notions like 'indiscretion', 'misdemeanour' and 'exception' are as predictable as they are morally vacuous. Experts may debate whether what happened in Batang Kai represents the customary conduct of war by the British Army, but that's little consolation to the victims and their families. 'Exceptionalism', while it exonerates the wrong-doers, has the power to transport the victims to an ethical no-man's-land. For those less given to the allure of Empire, the line between Britain's liberal standards and its conduct sometimes nefarious in colonial wars can be precariously thin.

THE BRITISH ARMY BECAME experts in counter-insurgency because of the Empire. In Queen Victoria's long reign, historian Bryon Farwell writes, 'there was not a single year somewhere in the world where her soldiers were not fighting for her and her Empire'.[18] The imperial wars were small wars. Small wars, however, did not mean unimportant or insubstantial in military commitment. In the view of one of its key proponents, Major-General Charles E. Callwell, small wars were brutal campaigns launched against rebellious natives who did not muster regular troops or use modern principles of war but deployed instead 'hit and run' tactics and the cowardly avoidance of direct battlefield confrontation. Callwell was a product of the Victorian age. Colonial racism underpinned his *Small Wars – Their Principles and Practice* first published in 1896,[19] a classic in the field of British counter-insurgency still widely read today. For him colonial rebels were 'savages' and 'morally inferior', and against such enemies regular troops and the use of maximum force were both necessary and sufficient. The contest employed not only the force of arms and technology, but also 'civilized standards'. Artillery and the Maxim machine gun – airpower had yet to be invented – would in most cases bring an imperial war to a victorious conclusion. Since imperial wars were fought between savagery and godliness, the side that used the 'moral force of civilization' would enjoy

---

18 Byron Farwell, *Queen Victoria's Little Wars*, New York: Harper & Row, 1972, p. 1.

19 1st edition: London: HMSO, 1898. On Callwell's influence on British military culture, see Daniel Whittingham '"Savage warfare": C.E. Callwell, the roots of counter-insurgency, and the nineteenth century context', *Small Wars & Insurgencies* 23(4–5), 2012, pp. 591–607.

an edge towards victory. It is as if 'cultural superiority', not the use of troops and artillery and the Maxim gun, won wars. The nature of small wars was lifted above pure firepower and military violence; what defined it were the level of European cultural supremacy and the 'emotional and moral' effects it had on the native rebels.[20]

Reading Callwell – and his intellectual heir Major-General Charles William Gwynn, who wrote *Imperial Policing*[21] – calls up the scene of some David Lean epic: imperial troops fanning out across the plain, the bombardment having ceased, as they go about the business of punitive raiding, torching houses and destroying crops and livestock, as Christopher Plummer as the colonel watches from the height with his entourage. For the British then with godliness on their side, the sense of military triumph was unmitigated by 'collateral damage', as we would say these days. Yet imperial policing had never been only about the destruction of the enemy and his support base. The primary aim was to set an example, to impress on the natives the government's willingness to use brute force to punish and terrorize.

The last years of the nineteenth century saw a series of successes in suppressing rebellions by colonial powers: the US operations in the Philippines, the French in Madagascar, the British campaigns against the unrest on the Punjab frontier in 1897–1898 and in the South African War against the Boers. The genius of Callwell-style imperial policing was in emphasizing the dual effects of military violence: to kill and to intimidate, to destroy and to instil awe. Callwell believed the 'savage tribes' must be taught a lesson. Harsh methods were justified because, as he puts it, '[U]ncivilised races attribute leniency to timidity ... [They] must be thoroughly brought to book and cowed or they will rise again.'[22] The success of small wars depended on military violence, but the key was the stinging 'emotional and moral effects' that imperial might had on the natives.

Small wars formed the backbone of twentieth-century British counterinsurgencies. As the world moved to a more enlightened time, British military violence became more moderate and disciplined, and burning homes and destroying crops and livestock an anachronism that neither the press nor public opinion was prepared to accept. In war, the British military code would usher

---

20 Ibid., p. 592.

21 London: Macmillan, 1934.

22 Callwell, *Small Wars*, p. 148, quoted in Daniel Whittingham 'Savage warfare', p. 594.

in the 'principle of minimum force' that reflected the new liberal values and ethical standards its armed forces should uphold. Under such a principle, 'The degree of force used in any policing situation – in Britain or abroad – had to be no more and no less than the minimum necessary to restore peace.'[23] As another war expert writes, quoting a 1923 Army manual,

> British soldiers have constantly been reminded that their task was 'not the annihilation of an enemy but the suppression of a temporary disorder, and therefore the degree of force to be employed must be directed to that which is secondary to restore order and must never exceed it'.[24]

In short, in Britain's counter-insurgencies its solders would behave nothing like the German Wehrmacht in its anti-partisan operations on the Eastern Front during the Second World War.

One way to view 'minimum force' is as an immutable legal precept that sets a 'clear standard against which the conduct of soldiers and police could be measured'.[25] In the various versions of the British military code, the basic tenet is this: the armed forces, when called up to aid civilian authorities, must employ the degree of force necessary 'to restore order and must never exceed it'. This is the legal basis on which a member of the armed forces using excessive force can be prosecuted.

However, soldiers in the field also face another legal military rule, one that tends to dilute a strict adherence to 'minimum force'. For alongside the prohibition of excessive force, soldiers can also be tried for using too little of it. Military regulations require a solder in a battle to be aggressive in attack and in defence. Often maximum rather than minimum force is demanded of them, and court martial awaits those deemed cowardly and lacking in the combative spirit. For the average soldier, the situation can be ambiguous and difficult as he faces the old question: 'Shall I be shot for my forbearance by a court martial, or hang for excess zeal by a jury'?

That question came from General Sir Charles Napier (1782–1853), conqueror of Sind and the British Army's commander-in-chief in India, who knew a thing or two about quelling colonial unrest. He expressed a dilemma that

---

23 Rod Thornton, 'The British Army and the origin of its minimum force philosophy', *Small Wars & Insurgencies*, 15(1), 2004, p. 87.

24 Thomas R. Mockatitis, 'The minimum force debate: contemporary sensibilities meet imperial practice', *Small Wars & Insurgencies* 23(4–5), 2012, p. 87.

25 Ibid., p. 763.

still haunts the average British soldier today. In the broadest sense, there is an inherent tension in asking a soldier drilled for violence and aggression to put his warrior hawkishness on the leash. In Afghanistan between 2001 and 2011, the sporadic abuse and killing of civilians by some NATO troops show how serious this can be. In a firefight quick decisions must be made, often in a matter of split seconds; only later can experts – and military tribunals – sit down, with the facts before them, and argue about what a soldier might or should have done. Looking at it this way, 'minimum force' comes across as the faultline of a military code that not infrequently puts a trooper in the field under stress.

In Malaya, even in the early Emergency years of 1948–51, the 'minimum force' rule was not altogether ignored. Abuses were nonetheless frequent. In the counter-insurgency the use of force went through a mutation, a noticeable shift. The government's earlier approach of 'screwing down the people' had seemed like lifting a chapter from *Small Wars*: a blending of direct military action and threat and intimidation. Now, the emphasis was on 'soft power' as the government increasingly turned the war on the civilians. The instruments were the law and the Emergency Regulations that gave the government a wide range of powers of arrest and imprisonment as well as banishment overseas of those charged. By January 1952 when the new High Commissioner Sir Gerald Templer arrived, police and military operations were supplemented, in a significant degree, by economic development and social welfare assistance – the winning of the 'hearts and minds' of the Malayan people.

The British High Commissioner Sir Henry Gurney was killed in an ambush in October 1951, gallantly drawing fire from his wife by creeping away from their Rolls-Royce as the MNLA guerrillas poured a hail of bullets into the car, so the legend goes. Appointed in October 1948, Gurney had been the last British chief secretary in Palestine. The High Commissioner's early years were marked by uncertain policies and military tactics. The poor coordination between civil authorities and the military and police drew much criticism, especially from the Malayan business sector. In response Britain dismissed the Police Commissioner Nichol Gray, another Palestine old hand, and brought in a new Director of Operations, General Sir Harold Briggs, in April 1950. Briggs became associated with a programme of massive population resettlement that bore his name – the Briggs Plan – that eventually turned the war around, 'an account for other pages of the book'.

In fact the relocation of villagers had been happening well before Briggs's arrival. Often people were moved into a resettlement camp after a military

Forced eviction and relocation of civilians from squatter settlements. (Source: photo still from film footage reproduced in the 1998 BBC documentary, 'Malaya - the Undeclared War', online at www. youtube.com/watch?v=pBRMRf0JVJc.)

operation; each camp was surrounded by barbed wire fences and watch towers, while police patrols ensured added security. On 19 October 1948, after a MNLA attack, some 5,000 people were evicted from Batu Arang, a coal mining area with a history of labour strikes and communist agitation. In the same month hundreds of squatters were removed from Sungei Siput and Tronoh, a small mining town in Perak state. In such operations the burning of homes was routine, and in November 1948 the destruction of homes and property of people in suspect areas was made legal.

Some officials treated the torching of villagers' homes as retaliation for the communists' own arson at the rubber estates and tin mines. Such measures occasionally produced evidence of the suspects' guilt and were thus made defensible. A telegram to the Secretary of State noted: 'Police and military raided an area near Rawang, Selangor. No opposition. Large stocks rice and prepared food found and removed. House burnt and ammunition heard exploding in them.'[26] These operations were very much throwbacks to the imperial policing of old. Burning down huts was justified on various grounds: suspicion of

---

26 Huw Bennett, 'A very salutary effect', p. 439.

aiding the enemy; the discovery of food stocks, hideouts, weapons and ammunition; encouraging villagers to resettle in 'clear areas'. The other purpose
was to deny insurgents aid and destroy their support base, a time-honoured
counter-insurgency measure.

However, the military measures were also to set an example, to show the
villagers the dire consequences of refusing to follow government orders. The
aim was to destroy and punish; but as in all counter-insurgencies, the government had in mind the need to demonstrate the violent potency of the security
forces. The elimination of enemies was important, so was the imposition of
governmental will on civilians. The aim was as much to achieve direct kills as
to brandish the government's iron will, a legacy of Callwell's 'small war'. The
'emotional and moral effects' of imperial wars, we recall, were not about building a cosy relationship with the natives; they were certainly not about scaling
down military violence. Terms like 'persuasion' and 'example setting' can take
on a gloss of official appeasement and reconciliation. However, for the civilians, threat and violence loomed behind any gestures of government benignity.

In the Emergency, troops and the police and home guards did what they
were supposed to do: destroy insurgents. But the government, especially after
the disastrous years of 1948–51, never forgot the lessons of Callwell–Gwynn
imperial policing. Military violence is important, more so the instilling of
awe and fear. The Emergency was fought on two fronts closely aligned: the
ambushes and jungle patrols that achieved enemy kills; and more pervasively
in daily life the translation of direct violence into *threat* in order to coerce and
intimidate the people. Much of this was achieved by the draconian Emergency
Regulations.

The Emergency Regulations provided the judicial framework that made
legal the various counter-insurgency measures.[27] Oppressions and restrictions
on a wide area of social life were made a matter of law. The harsh effectiveness
of the regulations can be gleaned from their details. The High Commissioner
could, with unrestricted right, make laws 'deemed desirable in the public interest and to prescribe penalties, including the death penalty'.[28] And the law gave
government the power of arrest, detention without trial, collective punishment,
and deportation and banishment. In ungainly legalese, the Emergency Regula-

---

27 R.D. Renick, 'The Emergency Regulations of Malaya: Causes and Effects' *Journal
of Southeast Asian History* 6 (2), pp. 1–39, for the baroque complexity and punishing effects.

28 Ibid., p. 17.

tions enabled the Chief Secretary to 'order a person to be detained without trial for a period not exceeding two years and at the end of the period, extend the detention for a further maximum of two years.'[29] After the declaration of the State of Emergency, between January and October 1949, more than a 1,000 undesirables were detained for interrogation each month. At the end of the year, some 5,363 persons were under detention and with them 213 dependents, mostly children. The tightening of the net expanded the prison population. To cope with the problem, the government created Emergency Regulation 17C which provided the High Commissioner with the power of deportation and banishment. The law affected Chinese and Indians, who were mostly immigrants. The official count for 1949 gave: 6,149 persons deported to China and 225 to India; Chinese deportees accompanied by 2,913 dependents; a total of almost 10,000 men, women and children.[30]

Detention and deportation could also be applied to a group of persons in an area. The notorious Regulation 17D made collective punishment legal. Under the regulation the High Commissioner could detain inhabitants of an area *if any of them* had committed the offences of: aiding, abetting, consorting with or harbouring persons who 'intending to act or who had acted in a manner prejudicial to the public safety or the public order'; suppressing evidence of offences; failing to give information or take 'reasonable steps to prevent the escape of any person they knew or had cause to know was a person intended to act or had acted in a manner prejudicial to the public safety or the public order'.[31] The regulation also prescribed deportation: 'Any person detained could be ordered to leave and remain out of the Federation by the High Commissioner in Council, provided they were not a Federal citizen or British subject'.[32] Appeal was not allowed for detention or deportation authorized under the Emergency Regulations.

17D was among the harshest of the Emergency Regulations. It produced its own catchment of victims. In 1949 some sixteen operations were carried out over wide areas and caught 6,434 people deemed to have committed offences listed under the regulation, of whom 740 were later deported to China.[33] In October 1949 the communists came to power in China. Chinese ports were

---

29 Ibid., p. 19.

30 Ibid., p. 22.

31 Ibid.

32 Ibid., p. 23.

33 Ibid., p. 22.

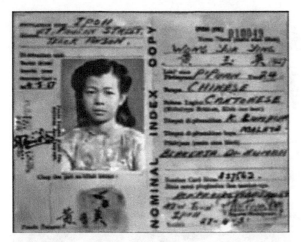

Identity card from the time of the Emergency (Source: photo still from the 2010 History Channel documentary, 'The Malayan Emergency', online at www.youtube.com/watch?v=HgUMXHsIfe8.)

closed to the disembarkation of deportees from Malaya. Hainan Island in the south was still in the Nationalists' hands for the remaining months of 1949, but it only admitted deportees who were native Hainanese. All this changed the pace of deportation, though the rate of detention remained unabated. In 1950, 8,508 persons were detained, accompanied by 527 dependents. A substantial number of these – 3,746 persons or about 40 per cent – were ordered to be deported, and 887 persons accompanied by 514 dependents left for China.[34]

Deportation eventually tapered off. The communist takeover of China was one reason. The other was population resettlement that moved people from areas outside government control into resettlement camps, the so-called 'New Villages'. Meanwhile deportation continued when it could. Many were offered the choice of 'voluntary repatriation' after receiving sentences of long imprisonment or death. Most accepted. China allowed the disembarkation of deportees from Malaya until late 1950. Overall the total number of Chinese deported throughout the Emergency numbered 26,000 persons; those who accepted voluntary deportation brought the figure to around 30,000.[35] The deportees suffered greatly socially and psychologically. Many were later prosecuted during the Cultural Revolution for their 'foreign connections'.

Not only to their victims did the laws of deportation and banishment come across as an exercise in massive cynicism. Malayan men and women were

---

34 Ibid.

35 Ibid., p. 23.

Australian soldier and Malayan policeman check the identity papers of an elderly man at a roadside checkpoint in Perak state, c. 1956. (Source: Australian War Memorial, HOB/56/0798/MC.)

deported to a 'homeland' that no longer was any such thing, and sending ex-insurgents to the newly established communist regime reeked of diplomatic dumping. But the British could also argue that deportation offered a more humane way out for long-term detainees, and allowed those sentenced to death to escape the gallows. In this sense banishment in exchange for imprisonment or death seemed a fair, ethical bargain. And the legal point about citizenship in Regulation 17D was observed. Malayan citizens could not be deported; but then local-born dependents who could claim citizenship by birthright invariably accompanied a deportee. At a time when the Emergency Regulations allowed for the passing of the death penalty for a variety of crimes of 'association with the communists terrorists', deportation could generously be construed as a gesture of British liberalism and decency.

Not only in regard to deportation could it be argued that the Emergency itself was inter-penetrated with the fairness of British rule and legal justice. For one thing, those given the death sentence could appeal to the Privy Council, which occasionally did overturn a ruling of the Malayan court. A major tenet of the British counter-insurgency had been that the government must observe the law and conduct itself accordingly. We are a long way from 'jungle bashing' and firefights and the burning of villagers' huts. But then, for the government, beating the insurgents had never been dependent on military operations alone; the basic principle was control and oppression on a broad social front. The Emergency Regulations helped to generate the psychology of threat that was the genius of imperial policing. The oppressive Emergency Regulations aside, we only need to mention the one official measure that most affected the average Malayan. The identity card – the accursed IC which we still carry in Malaysia today – was a means of control and surveillance. Any business dealings, any visit to a government office required the IC; and, of course, you handed your IC to the soldiers at the roadblock and waited meekly while they checked your face against the photo. You were nothing without an IC; and you could be literally caught dead without one during a security sweep in your village. An IC may now be a clumsy inconvenience, but then most Malayans, especially those in the countryside, experienced much more than that.

If anything, in Malaya the British approach to counter-insurgency showed a deep understanding of mass psychology and the subtle interplay of benevolence and brutality, reward and punishment. Callwell, always an ardent voice that expressed the dilemma facing British soldiers on the battlefield, had this to say about their difficulties:

> The regular army has to cope not with determinate but with indeterminate forces. The crushing of a populace in arms and the stamping out of widespread disaffection by military methods is a harassing form of warfare even in a civilised country with a settled social system: in remote regions peopled by half-civilised races or wholly savage tribes, such campaigns are most difficult to bring to a satisfactory conclusion, and are always most trying to the troops.[36]

The Malayan Emergency was a harsh and vicious affair. It is also true to say that the campaign was conducted with a philosophical attitude, an intransigent understanding of the 'racial other' at the core of imperial policing, which was key to British success.

---

36 See Huw Bennett, 'A very salutary effect', p. 596.

4 On Revolutionary War
Making peasants into revolutionaries

[War] is a trial of strength of the moral and the physical forces by means of the latter.... [T]he conditions of the mind have always been the most decisive influences on the forces employed in War.
– Carl von Clausewitz, *On War* (1832)

You know, Ali, it's hard enough to start a revolution. It's harder still to sustain it, and hardest of all to win it. But it's only afterwards, once we've won, that the real difficulties begin.
– 'The Battle of Algiers' (1966)

On a warm summer morning in November 1999 some forty academics and Malayan Emergency experts gathered in the cool, oceanic seminar room of the Australian National University in Canberra to meet the 75-year-old Chin Peng.[1] After the signing of the 1989 peace agreement, the MCP secretary-general lived in Thailand, overseeing the welfare of ex-MNLA men and women, and enjoying fame as an ex-leader of a communist revolution. A celebrity, he gave interviews and held court in his Bangkok hotel room, and these media pursuits eventually led to the invitation from the ANU to meet the academics. It was the only such meeting he ever attended; Chin Peng died in September 2013, so the two-day 'dialogue session' turned out to be a memorial of sorts for a remarkable man. When alive, he was already a monument of history on whom people of all shades and inclinations would write their ideas and discernments. The 'dialogue session' was held outside Malaysia, so it ignited no ideological flame; and those who took part were an objective, cool-headed lot, among them his former nemeses who, serving with Malayan police, had spent years pursuing him and trying to kill him off. In the gathering, denuded of ideo-

---

1   Published as C.C. Chin and Karl Hack, *Dialogue with Chin Peng: New light on the Malayan Communist Party*, Singapore: Singapore University Press, 2004.

logical contentions, questions were directed at Chin Peng about his life and his revolutionary career, his leadership of the MCP and the party's strategy at each stage of the Emergency. Thus preoccupied, the academics eschewed abstract, dialectical arguments of the type that might fire up a Mao or a Che Guevara. To their questions Chin Peng answered matter-of-factly, for he himself was not given to philosophy or the theory of revolution. At one point, the secretary-general was asked; 'How was it that, with MCP's strong position after the war, it was caught unprepared by the start of the Emergency?' He replied:

[T]he prominent factor that influenced us, when we decided to take up arms, was the British policy at that time. We felt we were being cornered, gradually, back to the corner. We had nowhere to move. Of course, the international factor played some role, but not as decisive ... After three years of peaceful struggle, even though we could succeed in mobilising the masses, to organise *hartal* (Malay public assemblies), general strikes and universal stoppages of shops and businesses.... We couldn't force the British Government to make concessions. So what is the usefulness of continuing a peaceful struggle? ... We had to make a formal review of this policy.[2]

It was a remarkable admission. Having infiltrated the labour movement and trade unions, the MCP had made little leeway on the political front. Faced with a series of strikes and labour unrests, the government responded with banishment and trespass laws against the offenders. The brutal repression caused the MCP to change tack by taking up the armed struggle. In the concluding session, Chin Peng made the same point about MCP's unpreparedness. At the opening of 1948, barely six months before the start of the Emergency, the party was still pitching for a policy of open, united-front politics in the cities.

All along we considered we were on the defensive side.... [At the time] we still considered how to further our peaceful struggle. We were still considering how to change our party from an underground status to an open, legal status....[O]nly at the end of January 1948, when we started to review our policy, then we had to stop all this, we cancelled all the plans.

And he ended laconically, 'You can say the decision [to turn to violent rural struggle] was taken in a hurry, in haste.'[3] We are caught with the implication:

---

2 Chin and Hack, *Dialogue with Chin Peng*, pp. 117–119.
3 Ibid., p. 135.

with its attention directed at the cities, the MCP had fallen short in preparing the ground for a rural guerrilla war.

IN COMMUNIST LEGEND THE retreat to the countryside exudes not defeat but revolutionary romance. Think of Castro and his 81 comrades. Having landed in Cuba they found sanctuary among the peasants in the mountains, and two years later in January 1959 the struggle they led brought down the Batista regime. Or think of the Chinese communists' withdrawal from Shanghai after the April 1927 massacre by Chiang Kai-shek's forces. For Mao the disaster was a vindication of his idea of a rural-based revolutionary struggle in China, an idea that had been the seed of his 'Report on an Investigation of the Peasant Movement in Hunan' (1927). The Shanghai massacre eventually pointed the way out of the cities and to the rural peasantry who became the *raison d'être* of the Chinese communist revolution. A new tactical and ideological shift, the retreat to rural China rewrote the textbook of revolutionary war in South East Asia.

Malayan communists like Chin Peng looked up to Mao and his idea of an agrarian-based revolution. (The MCP even called its hard slog from Pahang to the Betong Salient in Southern Thailand in 1953 the 'Long March.') It is, of course, difficult to compare Chin Peng's enterprise with that of Mao and his colleagues. The historical circumstances – not to mention the personal qualities of the two men – were vastly different. Nonetheless, Marxism had opted for the view of revolution as a 'science'; the communist struggle would follow a dialectical logic and be 'overdetermined' by historical and economic forces. Even the most naïve communist rebels couldn't do without the orthodoxy laid out by Marx, Engels, Lenin, Mao and other luminaries. Perhaps for this reason, a communist revolution always invites armchair, theoretical grilling by academic specialists. Regarding the MCP in the difficult year of 1948, there are some pertinent questions that go to the heart of matter. When the MCP was forced to take up arms, what were the conditions in the Malayan countryside which could be construed as presenting a 'revolutionary situation'? If so how was it to be exploited? And since the Maoist theory of rural guerrilla warfare looms large, who were the 'peasantry' that were to be the vanguard of the communist struggle in Malaya?

THE PRE-1948 DECISION ON united-front politics had been the brainchild of Chin Peng's predecessor, the legendary Lai Teck, alias Mr Wright. The story of Lai Teck's career is worthy of a political soap opera. Arrested by the Kempeitai, the much-feared Japanese military police, he turned double-agent by agreeing to work with them. After the war he threw in his lot with the new master when caught by the British intelligence in Singapore. Lai Teck's betrayal had led to the decimation of the MCP leadership by the Japanese; and later, directed by his British handler, he took the party on a path of urban labour activism and united-front strategies easily monitored by the police. When the MCP investigators began to close in, he absconded with the party funds and escaped. He was finally caught in Bangkok and executed by the MCP's Thai comrades: a grisly end to a pernicious career.[4]

The MCP was later to blame secretary-general Lai Teck for delaying the armed insurrection and pinning all hopes on political struggle in the towns and cities. But in 1945–7 everyone, not least the communists, was embroiled in the democratic experiment under the British Military Administration. The MCP and its front organizations operated openly. With the workers and students radicalized by the war, for a while the towns and cities seemed to offer the best chance of gaining power through mass mobilization and electoral politics.

The declaration of the Emergency in June 1948 saw most of the MCP leaders arrested and the party's infrastructure in the urban centres destroyed. With well-functioning transport and intelligence gathering, the colonial authorities targeted each 'communist subversive' on the police blacklist and made mass arrests. Unlike the kasbah in Algiers, the Chinatowns in Singapore and Malaya were no 'cities within cities' with densely packed houses and narrow alleyways where revolutionaries could set up clandestine cells without police detection. For the MCP the urban centres had become a trap.

In returning to the countryside the MCP's insurgents were again operating on familiar ground. During the Japanese occupation the MPAJA had enjoyed considerable support from the Chinese villagers. To them the MPAJA guerrillas were battling the Japanese devils who had raped and killed and burned their way across the ancestral homeland since the invasion of Manchuria in 1931; and in Malaya they had fought on while the 'white men' had run away and abandoned the people. In 1948 the war with Japan had been over for three years. For the Malayan Chinese, anti-Japanese resistance was one thing: it involved patriotism and the protection of the people. Fighting for a Socialist Malaya was something else. For those facing the more immediate tasks of rebuilding their homes and livelihoods, it sounded airily abstract. A great deal

---

4   Chin Peng gave his version of Lai Teck's treacherous career in Chin and Hack, *Dialogue with Chin Peng*, pp. 124–132.

of work was cut out for the MCP to convince them of the rightness of its cause. It would need to turn 'Malayan Socialism' into a rallying call for revolutionary struggle. It would have to transform the villagers into *revolutionaries*.

If the Malayan Emergency is the story of a communist uprising, it is also one about rural squatters, which tells about the social chaos brought about by the Japanese occupation, the workings of the tin mines and rubber plantations, and the competitive land use by different interests. There's nothing more illustrative of the 'squatter story' than what happened in the Kinta Valley in Perak state, where major tin mines were found as they are today.

THE KINTA VALLEY SITS in the dip between the River Kinta and its estuaries, bounded in west by the Kledang Range and the Main Range in the east. The Kledang Range reaches some 3,500 feet high, and the Main Range at more than 7,000 feet is home to the Malay Peninsula's highest peak, the Gunung Tahan. From the sources at the two ranges several rivers cascade down and feed into the River Kinta. The water continues its flow and joins the River Perak further south. The topography is one of mountain ranges covered in thick jungle and sky-scraping trees, and flat land intersected by a system of rivers. In this valley are found Ipoh, the capital of Perak, and other smaller towns – Sungei Siput, Gopeng, Batu Gajah, Taiping, names forever associated with the Emergency. And located here today are small townships that were once 'new villages' where more than 100,000 rural squatters were resettled during the fifties.[5]

For centuries Perak's rivers and their tributaries had laid down a rich tin ore alluvium – black, sandy grains easily mined by hand in shallow open pits. In the 1840s, after the find of rich tin ore deposits, Chinese capital began to invest in mining, attracting Chinese labourers in large numbers. By 1890 they numbered almost 60,000, whose labour in the wet, malarial waters was producing some 8,000 tonnes of tin, about 30 per cent of the total from the Malay states.

European interests were aroused by reports from Malaya. In 1881 the French established the first mine – combined with a bit of spying, it was rumoured – in Perak. Compared with the Chinese who relied on the simple tools of changkul and rattan baskets, European mines used high-pressure hydraulic

---

5 The intimate relations between the tin mines and the squatters are drawn from Francis Loh Koh Wah, *Beyond the Tin Mines: Coolies, Squatters and New Villages in the Kinta Valley, c. 1880–1980*, Singapore: Oxford University Press, 1988. See also: E.H.G. Dobby, 'Resettlement transforms Malaya: A case-study of relocating the population of an Asian plural society', *Economic Development and Cultural Change*, 1(3), 1952, pp. 164–189. A pickul – also spelled pikul – is 60.5 kilograms.

jets to break up the tin-bearing soil, and the ore was recovered from the sluice boxes elevated above ground. Large amounts of tin were lost with this method, which required a prodigious supply of water. By the arrival of the twentieth century European capital had switched to the more efficient modern dredges, a system of continuously rotating metal buckets that excavated the alluvium ore from the water-filled mine pits.

European capital had the advantage of new technology and economies of scale, and it enjoyed government support. By 1874 *de facto* indirect rule had been established in Perak. In the first two decades of the twentieth century, Britain firmed up many of its policies in the Malay states. The control of labour, the collection of tax revenue, and law and order eventually became British responsibilities. Chinese secret societies that traditionally enforced order and extortion among the indentured labour were banned, and the Protectorate of Chinese Affairs took over matters relating to the Chinese population. In administration, land straddled the intimate alliance of capital and the colonial state. Under British indirect rule, the Malay states strove to serve European capital by releasing lands locked in the arcane land tenure system and making them available for industrial use. By the 1920s, with the expansion of tin mining and the rising rubber industry, a large area of land, some cultivated, some jungle, was gazetted 'state land'.

Thinkers of a Marxist bent are wont to talk of 'the penetration of European capital' when describing the devastating effects of modern, capitalist production on the traditional economy. The metaphor of sexual rapaciousness seems to me just right. In the Kinta Valley, the arrival of modern European capital changed forever the world of Chinese labourers, agents and merchant-miners, and with that the customary social relationships in the mines. The most immediate effect was the rapid decline of Chinese labourers and small Chinese operators using changkul and panning baskets in open-cast mines. In the 1913–23 decade, Chinese labourers working in such mines dropped from 99,000 to less than 13,000. 1927 was a good year for tin, when its price rose to $144 Straits Dollars per pickul; by then some 48 dredges were operating in Perak state.[6] The back of Chinese miners was irrevocably broken. Mass unemployment and the cloud of social unrest began to cast a gloom on the horizon.

There had been market gardens in the Kinta Valley since the 1880s. The farms were tiny plots and scattered. Some cultivators held annual licences; most squatted on state land. They proved to be an anarchic lot for the government:

---

6   Loh, *Beyond the Tin Mines,* p. 76.

it was hard to collect fees from the licensees, and harder still to enforce health and sanitary regulations on the farms. But land could not be left idle. The more far-sighted officials saw the potential of the squatter-farms. They could supply the mines and estates with vegetables and other produce, and at a time of massive retrenchment market gardening could serve as a safety valve by absorbing the unemployed labourers. All this needed careful management. As those laid off turned to farming for their livelihood, illegal encroachment on state land also increased alarmingly. 'Squatters' became an administrative nightmare, and many were fined or expelled from the occupied land. For the farmers, the land administration was an important political lesson. Those who had applied for land licences encountered long and expensive bureaucratic dealings. And they discovered that the government was reluctant to release land for cultivation if it had 'mining potential', and that land licences were mostly given to Malays.

Pragmatism nonetheless made the authorities rethink. During the First World War and the subsequent economic slump, there had been serious food shortages and large volumes of food had to be imported. At the same time, the government could not fail to notice that the farmers illegally occupying state land had, without official assistance, cleared it for planting and keeping pigs and chickens. 1921 was a bad year for the rubber industry; prices fell and new planting virtually stopped. With the prospect of social unrest, there was talk of repatriating the unemployed to China. But more sympathetic officials argued that, if repatriation went ahead, industries would be deprived of workforce needed when economic prosperity returned. In the situation squatter farms once again served as the 'informal sector' of the economics textbook. Illegal cultivation of state land took in many of the retrenched workers during the economic downturn, and became a reservoir of labour as mines and plantations resumed production. The process set the pattern for the following decades, as the squatter-cultivators found themselves in a condition between studied neglect and administrative control. Squatter-farms were kept alive by the Great Depression of the 1930s. Later, during the Japanese occupation, food shortages and daily brutalities in the cities forced many people to the countryside, who took up farming on state forests and at the jungle fringes.

THE 'SQUATTER PROBLEM' RETURNED with the British reoccupation of Malaya. As the colonial authorities set about restoring law and order, one of their priorities was to rehabilitate the mines and return them to production. The Japanese in retreat had destroyed much of the machinery and dredges and the industry faced huge expenses in replacing them at a time when the costs of transport and fuel were rising. Nevertheless, mine rehabilitation did take place, and by 1950 production had reached almost 400,000 pickuls, doubling the figure of 1947, two years after the British return.

An increase in production did not imply more labourers, however. In 1950 the mines took in some 27,000 people, significantly lower than the annual average of 39,300 from 1930 to 1941.[7] Mechanization and improved efficiency had created less need for workers. With fewer employment opportunities, the squatter-farms became even more important for the homesteaders. At a time of economic uncertainty, it was wise to hang on to the land they were cultivating, whatever its legal status. And those who had fled here during the Japanese occupation began to think of their places as home and stayed on. As things settled back to normal, some went to work in the mines or in shops and factories in the nearby towns, leaving the farm to their families. The squatter-farms were growing into permanent, dispersed settlements.

In the chaotic war years, the squatter homesteads had spread and encroached on the mines, the rubber estates, the Forest Reserves and the Malay Reserves. Now the authorities went about to untangle the mess. They demanded the return of state land, and gave in to Malay pressure to evict the Chinese squatters from the Malay Reserves. Out of this a complex licensing scheme eventually emerged. In the Forest Reserves permits allowed only the growing of food crops – rice, vegetables, sweet potatoes – not non-essentials like tobacco and tapioca for which, as the farmers knew, forest land was more suitable. The squatters could now apply for a Temporary Occupation Licence (TOL) that gave the farmers tenancy rights for a specific period. In the rubber estates the landowners were persuaded to retain the squatter-farmers for two years, giving them a short reprieve.

To enforce these measures, evictions were carried out, and offenders often put up a stiff resistance. They tried to delay evictions and demanded compensation for the crops and buildings left behind: illegal occupation of land was becoming a hot political issue. A squatter was defined by as one not having a government permit or licence for the land he was cultivating. But such legal niceties were often meaningless when, as time went by and with a growing family, he no longer viewed himself as a squatter, as a temporary homesteader ready to pack up and leave when the police came with an eviction order. The farm was home and security, from which people left for work when work was available, and a place of respite during times of economic downturn. By 1948

---

7   Ibid., p. 122.

at the start of the Emergency there were an estimated 400,000 such squatter-farmers and their families in the whole of Malaya, with about one-third of them in the Kinta Valley.[8]

As with elsewhere in Malaya, the 'squatter problem' in the Kinta contained a complexity far beyond the issue of the illegal occupation of state land and the farmers' need to hold on to their homes. For the government, the nuisance each farmer had created was half-compensated for by his usefulness; and the situation enjoyed a degree of official blessing when 'land encroachment' turned idle land to productive use. This was to change with the Emergency.

For the communists, the 'squatter-problem' seemed to have come out of a guerrilla-warfare manual. When the MCP was forced to retreat to the countryside after the start of the Emergency, it found among the homesteaders at the jungle fringes something like a 'revolutionary situation'. For here in the Kinta were the perennial causes that inflamed peasant revolts everywhere: land, land use and ownership. In the honeymoon period of 1945–7, when the MCP had operated as a legal organization, it had built its influence through a myriad of youth leagues, women's associations and social and cultural clubs. The Perak Mining Labourers Union (PMLU) and the Perak Rubber Workers' Union (PRWU) mobilized the workers and agitated for better wages and working conditions, and the tasks of giving the farmers a political voice and resisting eviction fell on the shoulders of the Perak Farmers Association, the Perak Sago Labourers Union and the Perak Forest Workers Union. These organizations enjoyed considerable popular support; the PMLU and the PRWU alone had 8,000 members.[9] To the communists, it seemed written in the stars that they could foment a revolution in the Kinta. Nor were they indulging in self-delusions. During the Japanese occupation the settlers had provided comfort and support for the MPAJA, whose Fifth Independent Regiment, was operating in the Bidor Hills south of Ipoh. Founded in December 1942, it had transformed itself from a small band of 80 young Chinese, armed with rifles abandoned by the retreating British soldiers, to a well-trained, fully equipped group of 800 fighters with 1,200 in reserve. The Regiment's claim on history came from its remarkable alliance with Force 136, the stay-behind party after the British

---

8   Kernal Singh Sandhu, 'The saga of the "squatter" in Malaya', *Journal of Southeast Asian Studies*, 5(1), 1964, p. 150

9   Loh, *Beyond the Tin Mines*, p. 178.

surrender.[10] During their sojourn in the Malayan jungle, Force 136 officers like John Davis, J.P. Hannah and Spencer Chapman enjoyed the sanctuary and protection of the communists. Spencer Chapman in his *The Jungle is Neutral*[11] was full of praise for the discipline and magnificent turnout of the regiment. Chin Peng was a political and liaison officer of the Regiment. After the war, Perak was recognized as the most important centre of anti-Japanese resistance, where the MPAJA had been best organized. It looked like a Maoist-style peasant guerrilla struggle could be waged in Kinta and potentially Malaya-wide.

THE TROUBLE IS THAT the Malayan–Chinese farmers were not quite peasants in the conventional sense. In academic thinking, peasants were usually tagged as stubbornly traditional and individualistic in outlook, whose world extended no further than the family, the village and the land they tilled. They ate what they sowed and were more or less economically self-sufficient. In truth, even in remote areas peasants also faced a set of structural relations with the wider world. Often what the peasants had in common was more than their traditional way of life. Their 'social sharing' included the social conditions that were age-old grievances: usurious landlordism, corrupt government officials and police, generations-old exploitation. For the communist guerrillas the life and grievances of the peasants were nascent ground for political agitation and mobilization, as the mainland Chinese communist movement had brilliantly shown.

In any case, this self-contained, socially coherent peasantry was a romantic fiction. Only in certain conditions, for example tribal groups deep in the forest, do such rural societies exist. As for the revolutionary potential of peasants, one must be sceptical of an easy understanding of the squatter-farmers as a vanguard of the communist struggle in Malaya. On this issue, Marx's view on the revolutionary potential of the peasant is not exactly complimentary. In *The Eighteenth Brumaire of Louis Bonaparte*,[12] he sees the French peasantry nineteenth century as deeply entrenched in the bourgeois institutions and legal system. Over time, the French peasants had been gradually changing from more or less self-sufficient family-based producers to commercial farmers. As small rural

---

10 For the best account of Force 136 operating with the Fifth Independent Regiment in Japanese-occupied Malaya, see Spencer Chapman, *The Jungle is Neutral*, London: Chatto and Windus, 1950; John Cross, *Red Jungle*, London: The Quality Book Club, 1957.

11 See note 10.

12 Moscow: Progress Press, 1937.

entrepreneurs, Marx shows, they tended to look beyond and cast their economic vision and political loyalty to beyond their social world. The result was that the farmers exhibited little or no inter-relationships within the community. Solidarity was like sand running through the fingers. Each farmer was for himself and his interests. Marx famously describes the French peasantry as 'a sack of potatoes'.

Modern peasantry, as anthropologists would observe, are not strong on social solidarity either. At best it is a matter of degree. In *Uncommon People: resistance, rebellion and jazz*, the historian Eric Hobsbawm wants us to think of peasants, rather than being locally bound and organically conservative, as connecting in various ways to other social groups within the community as well as to groups and institutions in the world beyond.[13] In a clear echo of *The Eighteenth Brumaire*, Hobsbawm eschews the idea of a homogeneous, unified peasant society. In his view, the peasant community is made up of a web of interlinkages, fanning out from its own class to other social collectivities, to social and political superiors, to other peasants in the next village, to the market town, and at the furthest to the government and the nation-state.

Hobsbawm's take on *The Eighteenth Brumaire* offers some interesting insights into the 'squatter-farmer problems' in colonial Malaya. One of the perplexing things about the MCP is that, for all the political support it garnered from its wartime reputation and labour activities, the rural struggle it led rapidly collapsed once the government began to tighten the screws on the countryside. We must ask: Why? The conventional answer is that this was brought about by the tough, effective government responses. To beat the communists, Briggs foresaw a military operation of 'rolling the map up on the guerrillas from bottom to top [of the Peninsula]',[14] but the major cause for the government success was a population resettlement that effectively denied food and support for the insurgents. Inside the New Villages, the Min Yuan network kept up its activities, offering easy prey to the Special Branch and army patrols. The fact is that the concentration of farmers in compact New Villages spelled the beginning of the end of the communist insurrection. Under government protection, the squatter-farmers tended to shift their allegiances. We must ask: Why did the villagers, the foundation of the MCP guerrilla struggle, so quickly lose their 'revolutionary fervour'?

There have been several answers to this. The most common one is that the Chinese were natural fence-sitters. They went over to the government's side

---

13 Eric Hobsbawm, *Uncommon People: resistance, rebellion and jazz*, London: Abacus Press, 1999.

14 Robert O. Tilman, *Asian Survey*, 6(8), 1966, p. 411.

A wounded insurgent being held at gunpoint after his capture, 1952. (Source: photo still from film footage reproduced in the 1998 BBC documentary, 'Malaya - the Undeclared War', online at www. youtube.com/watch?v=pBRMRf0JVJc.)

because it proved to be the more realistic provider of security; the implication is that they could have easily accepted the MCP if the communists had been able to offer a similar or better protection from government abuses. The 'fence-sitter' argument, for me anyhow, tends to make the villagers into supreme rationalists, like modern day consumers facing a purchasing choice. The other explanation is that Chinese villagers were culturally pragmatic people infallibly drawn to material needs and rewards. This argument is often extended to make sense of the behaviour of insurgents. Some Emergency experts are puzzled by the fact that Malayan Chinese guerrillas, once captured, were notoriously willing to 'sing' and betray their former comrades. Ideological avidity was quickly exchanged for 'captured dead or alive' rewards. Chinese cultural traits help to explain why 'bribing the reds to give up' was easy, as one expert puts it.[15]

These lines of reasoning come across as somewhat facile. 'Chinese culture' explains too much; and it belittles what is at the heart of any communist revolutionary movement: class consciousness and class ideology.

---

15 Kumar Ramakrishna, '"Bribing the Reds to give up": Rewards policy in the Malayan Emergency', *War in History*, 9(3), pp. 332–353, 2002.

The ground of rural guerrilla warfare is brittle. Cross-border aid and sanctuary, the ideological and material support of friendly powers, and, lest we forget, the chanciness of history – all sway the fortunes of insurgents and the cause they fight for. For Mao a revolutionary movement must also take on an existential tint: it must guide the struggle to the realm of culture and deep-seated customs and values. A 'struggle of culture' was to clarify and sharpen the aims and strategies of his revolution, and in the process lodge an 'ideological soul' in the heart of the communist movement. His *On Guerrilla Warfare* is full of urgings for 'a precise conception' and 'the study and comprehension' of the political goals of the anti-Japanese war, not only among the troops but also the peasants.[16] The peasants' class consciousness was to arise from the knowledge of their own experiences of injustice and oppression. Mao was wont to romanticize the peasantry, of course. Nonetheless it was his talent to see the foundation of Chinese communism as built upon the perennial needs and grievances of the peasants. The revolution was nothing without them – the injustices they endured and the means to address them.

Yet even Mao himself recognized that the peasantry did not naturally exist as the fount of revolution. It required a great deal of 'political work' – always a mixture of persuasion and coercion – to transform the peasants into revolutionaries. His path-breaking *Report on an Investigation of the Peasant Movement in Hunan*, written in 1927, called on the CCP to cede the major revolutionary role to the peasants, not to the urban proletariat as in orthodox Marxism.[17] The *Report*, in arguing for the historical role of the peasants, brought to the fore 'the ways of raising class consciousness' – organizing farmers' cooperatives and associations, encouraging 'bans and prohibitions' on opium-smoking and gambling, extending schools and learning to the farmers. And he impressed upon the reader the 'fundamental spirit and revolutionary significance' of these ways.[18] The 'objective conditions' that defined the Hunan peasantry as a class were easily recognized by the then-young Mao, but it was the 'cultural work' that would instil in the peasants the will, the resolution, to rally to the revolutionary call.

In pre-communist rural China as in the Malayan countryside, farmers formed a class with a distinct social and economic character. In both rural situations, communist leadership faced the similar task: to inject, to fire up, a class consciousness among the peasants who were already *objectively* a class. This would

---

16 Mao Tse-tung, *Selected Works*, vol. IX, Peking: Foreign Languages Press, 1968.

17 Mao Tse-tung, *Selected Works*, vol. I, Peking: Foreign Languages Press, 1968.

18 Ibid., p. 29.

be a kind of confidence-building. The peasants, illiterate and mired in poverty, would be made to feel that they could raise the flag of struggle against those who had ground them down. The task was to transform the peasants' class relations into a mode of revolutionary consciousness. In Marxist terms, the fact of 'class in itself' – a class existing in a structural relation with the wider political economy – had to be elevated to the level of 'class for itself'. The condition of 'class for itself' existed when the peasantry were radicalized and made aware of their revolutionary potential, their role as the wellspring of communist rural struggle.

In revolutionary war theoretical questions invariably touched on practical ones. The issues of class and class consciousness deeply informed the tactics and long-term strategies of a communist movement. Revolutionary consciousness could also 'do' a great deal, alongside guns and grenades. The consciousness of a 'class for itself' would build the ramparts against defeatism when the revolution's fortune was at its lowest; just it would sustain people's hope when all seemed lost. Class consciousness could in practice be articulated in the steadfastness of revolutionaries. When captured, they might choose martyrdom rather than the betrayal of their comrades: communists at their most ideologically devout. Class-inspired ideology could maintain discipline and enable the tough to get going when the going got tough. To the question regarding the fickleness of the Chinese squatter-farmers and the MNLA insurgents, the answer may be one about the depth of a revolutionary consciousness that could help to blunt the force of government punishment and reward. From the point of view of revolutionary strategy, that a situation of 'class in itself' had existed among the Kinta farmers guaranteed nothing. Hobsbaum may well be speaking of colonial Malaya when he asks,

> Objectively [the peasantry] can be defined as a class 'in itself' in the classical sense, namely, a body of people who have the same kind of relation to the means of production . . . But how far is it a 'class for itself' – a class conscious of itself as such?'[19]

MCP leaders like Chin Peng had no doubt read their Mao and knew the communist folklore about the rural guerrilla warfare in China. All the same, when Chin Peng admitted to the MCP's unpreparedness when forced into a military struggle, he implicitly brought up one of the key causes for the insurrection's collapse.

In the Kinta Valley, once the Emergency Regulations were in place, the squatter-farmers faced government repressions no less severe than the insur-

---

19 Hobsbawn, *Uncommon People: resistance, rebellion and jazz*, p. 34.

gents. For the security forces, evicting the homesteaders and torching their huts reversed the Maoist guerrilla warfare dictum by 'draining the water that sustains the fish'. Government measures and population resettlement proved to be remarkably effective. In spite of the MCP's own claim, army and police patrols slowed to a dribble the flow of food and aid to the insurgents, and once inside the barbed wire fences of the New Villages those still willing to support them could do very little.

Marx's French peasantry as a 'sack of potatoes' suggests a transitionary stage in their continuous evolution. As rural producers who were making a bid for bourgeois institutions and values, they were yet to become aware of their own interests *in relation* to those who dominated and exploited them. Theirs was a world of expansive connections, connections that undermined their own perception of themselves as a body of people with their own economic and political destiny. The French peasantry were yet to become a class 'for itself'. Can we say that a similar situation existed among the squatter-farmers in postwar Malaya?

As the Japanese occupation ended, so did the need of the self-sufficient, green sanctuary of the Chinese homesteaders. What happened, however, was not the death of squatter-farming but its transformation. All manner of factors – the restoration of the Malayan economy, the food shortage, the growth of market towns – turned the cultivators into small commercial farmers. It is easy to imagine, over time, a band of wholesalers' lorries fanning across the countryside to reach the farmers, and conveying their produce to the urban markets. As the farmers took up work in the mines and estates in the rise and ebb of employment opportunities, they verged towards becoming a 'rural working class'. To me, 'rural working class', rather than the clumsy 'squatter-farmers', better captures the social complexities of these family-based agrarian producers cum mine and estate workers. The fact is that, as geographer Kernal Singh Sandhu puts it, 'in the post-war period, the squatters changed from producing chiefly for themselves to being commercial farmers'.[20] With their twin class identities – as farmer-producers and as industrial workers – there was no escape from the conditions of their multiple allegiances that increasingly hauled their world to beyond their homes at the jungle fringes.[21] The Emergency came, and the

---

20 Sandhu, 'The sage of the "squatter" in Malaya', p. 150.

21 Ray Nyce describes the social connectedness of squatter-farmers in the Cameron Highlands in Ray Nyce, *Chinese New Villages in Malaya: A community study*, Singapore: Malaysian Sociological Research Institute, 1973.

communists made their visits as they had done during the Japanese times, but the farmers were not so isolated as not to know that times had changed. With the cunning nurtured by years of making do on land they did not own, having lived by their wits in an economy given to periodic uncertainty, they could conceivably ask themselves: How can kicking out the British create a better livelihood for us? And what has socialism got to do with us, when all things considered we are not doing too badly?

There was the land ownership issue, of course. With the bodies of slain insurgents heaped outside the police stations or laid out in the market square, not only the most astute and pragmatic would have realised this: it was the starched-shirted British and Malayan officers, not the communists, who would help them to sort out the bureaucratic mess. And as the Malayan Chinese Association (MCA), the ethnic Chinese party of the Malay–Chinese–Indian coalition in the takeover government, began to extend its influence to the countryside, grievances were best channelled to the prominent men of the Anglo-Chinese elite. The squatter-farmers were quickly learning how to exploit the new circumstances. When the MCP were expelled deeper and deeper into the jungle, when the expanding web of influences and connections started to affect their lives, the rural producers never flowered into the Marxist 'class for itself' and all that it implied politically.

In any conflict the victor may boast about his talent and brilliant strategic vision, but the enemy's failings are a part of the reason for his success. For insurgents, patience is a prime virtue. Luck and political environment permitting, success in many cases is granted to those who have, over decades, borne the brunt of blood and sacrifice and have prepared the ground. I don't want to sound like a Cold War warrior, but the failings of the MCP were many. To say that in 1948 it was caught unprepared by the start of the Emergency is to open up the historical reckoning that hamstrung the communist revolution in Malaya, something too often glossed over by communist leaders like Chin Peng. We are certain, for example, that not all squatter-farmers willingly and wholeheartedly put themselves behind the wheel of the communist cause. In the early years of the Emergency, there were plenty of insurgent attacks on buses and trains; and civilians suffered when grenades were tossed into crowds and coffee shops, and their livelihoods were destroyed when mine machinery was sabotaged and rubber trees slashed. Goodwill was irreversibly damaged when people read about – or witnessed – the guerrillas dispatching a rubber tapper or an informant by tying him to a tree and cutting his throat or slicing open his belly, then leaving the body for others to find.

Something else also stood in the way of turning the squatter-farmers into revolutionaries. Driven by the need to make good in their new home, immigrants do not eagerly join the revolutionary crowd and man barricades in the streets. The Malayan jungle homesteaders were often immigrants of some one or two generations back. Imbued with the values and aspirations of an 'immigrant culture', they laced their buoyant economic hope with a sense of life's ill-guardedness and uncertainty. This is probably the core of their pragmatism: in their minds what communism could offer had to be laid against the more intractable problems that defined the horizons of their existence. The MCP made a great deal of its struggle as a 'rice-bowl revolution', one that would lead to economic security for all. But what measures could the MCP implement that would give solidity to such a promise? For there was nothing like land reform, land redistribution or the village 'struggling sessions' as in rural China that the MCP could offer to pepper up people for the revolutionary cause. With a large chunk of the Malayan countryside dominated by the kampungs of Malay-Muslims, a colonial power determined to protect its business assets, a Chinese population trying to make good on their own terms – all this made a fantasy of a Maoist rural uprising in Malaya. For all the talk of 'poor class consciousness' among the squatter-farmers, the MCP's own incompetence may turn out to be most decisive after all.

And then there was the seductive pull of history. In the 1999 ANU dialogue, Chin Peng again and again pointed to what had happened internationally and to the conditions at home that seemed to his ilk to make for a ripe revolutionary situation. In the context of the communist successes in China and Vietnam, the rising strength of the Communist Party of Indonesia (PKI) and the wave of nationalist struggles in other colonies, a meek MCP inaction could have risked missing the history boat for the communists. Chin Peng is not alone in this regard; the twentieth century is full of revolutionaries who misjudged their historical conditions. From Fanon's endorsement of revolutionary violence – 'Europe has laid her hands on our continents, and we must slash at their fingers till she lets go'[22] – to Che Guevara's miserable end in the jungle of Bolivia, they share a story of clandestine gloom, effective government counter-terror, and over-exuberant, unjustified revolutionary hope.

---

22 Jean Paul Sartre, Preface to Frantz Fanon, *Wretched of the Earth*, New York: Grove Press, 1963, p. 12.

5 On 'Hearts And Minds' – I
'A warm and fuzzy war'

When we speak about 'Hearts and Minds', we are not talking about being nice to the natives, but about giving them the firm smack of the government.
– Hew Strachan, 'British counter-insurgence from Malaya to Iraq' (2007)

Since the war, our methods, our techniques, that is, and those of the communists are becoming very much the same. I mean occasionally we have to do wicked things. Very wicked things indeed.
– John le Carré, *The Spy Who Came In From the Cold* (1963)

Most people in Malaysia, if they look far back enough, have a story to tell about the Emergency. My father, who ran a Chinese herbal shop in High Street, Kuala Lumpur, in the late fifties, lived in security and comfort in the city, but even his life was touched by the insurgency. Overworked and having contracted tuberculosis, he once spent three months recuperating in the Lady Templer Hospital, named after the wife of General Sir Gerald Templer, High Commissioner and Director of Operations of Malaya in the critical years of 1952–54. (Peggy Templer was also the head of the Malayan Red Cross, among her other charity work.) In a photograph taken just before he was discharged, my father sits up on the bed, newspaper and glasses on his lap, his face beaming with good health. He would die twelve years later in 1967, from a heart attack, the effect of stress from working ten hours a day, seven days a week, at a cut-throat small business in Kuala Lumpur. Now in the photograph he is contentment itself, and to him the Lady Templer Hospital that restored him to health was the blessing of British rule. 'What would Malaya be if it were still in the hands of the Malays and their Sultans?', he once said to me. But then my father always had good things to say about the British – it was he who taught me the expression, 'The sun never sets on the British Empire', sounding mangled and

77

briskly cacophonous in the Hakka dialect of my family. In Malaya people could make a decent living and they were cared for when fallen sick, he would say. I know he was also thinking about China when he said it. As a wealthy landlord he and his family were put through the 'struggling sessions' during the land reform, and he had escaped by the skin of his teeth after paying a huge fine and having his land and property confiscated. So his pro-British views were bolstered by trimmings of anti-communism. When he went to the hospital in 1955, Templer had left Malaya in triumph and my father was insistent in his praise of the British. It felt like good fortune, with the colonial government in charge, to be living in Malaya.

British rule was many things to many people, however. It bore upon their lives in different ways. For all my father's enthusiasm for the Empire, the Emergency would catch up with him a surprising, unpleasant way.

One busy morning a man rang the shop, and speaking in Mandarin ordered sixty dozen of Johnson and Johnson cotton bandages; they were to be delivered to a coffee shop in Kajang New Village where he would be waiting. The man's voice was slow and steady, almost thoughtful, and he did not haggle, just wanted to make sure the goods were not out-of-date and delivered on time. My father's mercantile instinct was baited. The next day he had the goods loaded onto his Volkswagen Kombi van and drove to meet the buyer. At the coffee shop a man came over and made himself known: 'I am the one who called you. Do you have the goods with you?' He was in his twenties, my father would later recall, his face and forearms sun-dyed a darkolive, the front of his khaki shirt spattered with dirt-spots. Nothing strange about the man, my father had thought, just a small merchant and part-time farmer, one who kept a sundry store in a plantation or a mine. They went over to the van. My father slid open the door, and the man, stooping his head, stepped in and opened one of the brown cartons. Satisfied, he got out and next a wad of fifty-dollar bills was handed over to my father. My father wanted to say something to mend the awkward silence, but the man was already walking away. A few minutes later, he came back with a heavy old Raleigh bicycle, roped down the cartons on the pillion at the back, and peddled off.

My father had little time to rejoice over the killer deal, however. A couple of days later two Special Branch men came the shop and asked for him. My father served them tea and tried his charm, but they kept to their stony faces. He had aided the communists, the detectives told him; the man at the coffee shop was a Min Yuen agent. My father had sold the bandages to the communists and he was to accompany the detectives to the police station for questioning. At this point the family legend gets into a muddle. The joke is about my father turning into a communist sympathizer, a point of acute irony in view of his experience in Red China. But there is no hilarity in the rest of the tale. He was held at the High Street Police Station for one day and one night, and he never talked about what happened. It was his first and last brush with the law in Malaya and he wanted to keep the whole thing to himself.

Still, the idea did come to me: he was a well-respected, law-abiding person, and the incarceration must have cost him his dearly. My father, the criminal! I think of him in the dank cell with others with more prominent criminal careers. Did the purse-snatcher boast about his own profitable ventures? Did a fellow communist suspect pour out his woes about the injustice being done to him and his family? And I wanted most to know: Did my father secretly in his heart modify his fawning subservience to the colonial authorities after that? I never found out the answers to these questions. Outwardly at least, his view on the benevolence of British rule never wavered.

I feel distinctly unfilial when I tag my father as petty bourgeois and a complicit colonial. That's not the point of the story, though. Since he was a man of his time, when colonialism, in many people's minds, had brought peace and prosperity to Malaya, who is to say his view was wrong? The British the bringers of wealth and law and order: it was an enticing idea that won the hearts and minds of the likes of my father. His attitude may have been one of the classic 'shopkeeper' – conservative, self-interested and supportive of the status quo, but he was also being pragmatic. An immigrant, he had created a life of modest comfort for himself and his wife and seven children, and you can't blame him for believing that only the lazy and the weak-minded would not make it in this place of wise rule and benevolent government. The communists too promised a better life. But their 'rice-bowl revolution' was tied in with other aims he couldn't get the drift of – anti-imperialism, nationalism and socialism that was, if he recognized it, an echo of the murderous nightmare he had experienced in China. In contrast, British rule was practical and immigrant- and business-friendly. Unlike with communism, you didn't have to wait for the future; the good life was already here.

Whence came his sense of realism? In colonial rule, official interests were often meshed with the needs and aspirations of the native stakeholders. Obeisance came easily to those who had built their lives in a colony. For my father, it was not much of a choice between peace and prosperity under the government and the socialist paradise of the communists. Only the foolhardy would not back the side that delivered so much. And my father was not alone in holding such an amicable view on the Empire.

General Sir Gerald Walter Robert Templer served as Malaya's High Commissioner and Director of Operations between 1952 and 1954. As well as taking decisive control of operations against the insurgency, he worked hard to win the hearts and minds of ordinary Malayans. (Source: photo still from film footage reproduced in the 2010 History Channel documentary, 'The Malayan Emergency', online at www.youtube.com/watch?v=HgUMXHsIfe8.)

IN MARCH 1952 MALAYA had a new High Commissioner. The previous one, Sir Henry Gurney, had been killed in a communist ambush on his way to Fraser's Hill, a popular hill station in Pahang state. General Sir Gerald Templer had long experience in military intelligence and had served for a time as Director of Military Government in postwar Germany. He was, as they say, tailored for the job. Churchill when appointing him called Templer 'one of the scrappiest fighters and toughest administers in the British army'.[1] Templer had begun his career on the Western Front in 1916, and had served in the Caucasus against the Bolsheviks in 1919, in Palestine against the Arab revolt in 1935, and at Dunkirk in 1940. His reputation was formidable, and colourful. When as Britain's military governor in occupied Germany, on hearing that army clerks were making snide remarks doubting the stories of genocide at Belsen, he had sent them over to the concentration camp and ordered them to shovel corpses as punishment.[2] *Time* magazine reported his 'firmed appointment', and observed that his 'forthright methods should go far toward bringing order out of the chaos in Malaya's jungles'.[3]

---

1   John Cloake, *Tiger of Malaya: The life of Field Marshal Sir Gerald Templer*, London: Harrap, 1985, p. 262.

2   Ibid., p. 125.

3   *Time Magazine*, 15 December 1952, p. 7.

Templer was appointed High Commissioner and Director of Operations, the top civil and military posts in Malaya. It was the first time in modern colonial Malaya such a dual appointment had been made. The idea was that by concentrating the two powers in one man, government actions would be better coordinated; there would be no more of 'the left hand not knowing what the right hand was doing'. Only in a dictatorship are the powers of both the government and the military invested in one person. But this was an unusual time for Malaya, and the country was fighting a tough insurgency. Templer has his fans among historians, who credit him with turning the Emergency around by pushing for winning the 'hearts and minds' of the rural Chinese and bringing them over to the government's side.[4] In this narrative, Templer's arrival stopped the rot, and brought to an end the confusion and indecisiveness of the Gurney years (1948–51).

In this version, the government's failure had several causes. The lack of strong leadership and government resolve was one, poor intelligence and an inexperienced police force another. Added to these was a government ill equipped to quell the violence of the MNLA guerrillas. In the first six months of the Emergency there had been more than 200 incidents of communist attacks and sabotage. In the towns, assassination squads targeted police officers and informants in revenge attacks. The MNLA's ability to strike at will shocked the European business interests, especially the planters and miners. Templer's arrival brought a sense of relief. He tightened the Emergency Regulations, intensified intelligence gathering, and boosted the training of troops and police. The resettlement and regrouping of squatter-farmers had been completed, and now Templer would turn the New Villages into a 'battleground' in which food denial, collective punishment and the winning of hearts and minds were to be carried out.

Templer was a showman, shrewd in the use of propaganda and public relations. In the newspapers and the Malayan Film Unit newsreels, the High Commissioner was always on the go, with journalists and photographers in tow wherever he went. As the Chief Scout of Malaya, he would, in khaki shorts and a shirt adorned with badges, give talks and make his rounds among the Cubs and Scouts in the country. Next he would be in a Malay kampung

---

4   See, for example, Kumar Kumakrishna, '"Transmogrifying" Malaya; The impact of Sir Gerald Templer (1952–54)', *Journal of Southeast Asian Studies*, 32(2), 2001, pp. 79–92; Richard Stubs, *Hearts and Minds in Guerrilla Warfare: the Malayan Emergency 1948–1960*, Singapore: Oxford University Press, 1989.

Heavily laden men of the Royal Australian Regiment move through a rubber plantation as they hunt Communist insurgents in Perak state, c. 1956. Australian and other Commonwealth troops were an essential part of the British war effort. (Source: Australian War Memorial, HOB/56/0495/MC.)

inspecting the Women's Home Guard – a photo of the visit shows him chatting to the women, each with a headscarf and dressed in a white blouse and floral sarong, a bandolier of shotgun cartridges around the waist. Impatient to get things done, he would turn up in a New Village to check on the progress of a school building or a water supply, and finding it delayed or of shoddy standard would phone the officer in charge at the Public Works Department to give him a serious dressing down.[5] All this built up his reputation and lent his leadership charisma and vigour. To his promoters Temper was 'the Tiger of Malaya' who saved Malaya at a critical juncture of the Emergency.

---

5   Cloake, *Tiger of Malaya: The life of Field Marshall Sir Gerald Templer*, p. 278.

Yet, the truth is that a good deal had been achieved by the time of his arrival. The government had consolidated its powers through the Emergency Regulations, which imposed a police state on Malaya. The military and the police enjoyed wide powers of search, arrest and detention; and the Emergency Regulations allowed draconian measures of curfews, restriction on public assembly, food control and collective punishment. Along with detention – by the end of 1949 the detention camps held 5,362 people – there was large-scale deportation of mostly Chinese, over 10,000 in 1949.[6] The government also introduced laws that imposed the death penalty for a number of offences, including the possession of firearms and explosives. The size of the security forces was substantially increased. By 1951 the security forces reached the peak of 40,000 British and Commonwealth troops, almost 67,000 police including Special Constables, and more than 250,000 Home Guard.[7] Following his appointment in April 1950, the Director of Operations, General Harold Briggs, had introduced major reforms that had put the government on a solid war footing. He strengthened the Information and Psychological Services, bringing Hugh Greene, the brother of the novelist Graham Greene and a future Director General of the BBC, to head it.

FOR THOSE OUTSIDE ACADEMIC circles, whether Templer actually turned the Emergency war around is perhaps less interesting than the methods he employed. Templer was a shrewd practitioner of the British art of counter-insurgency. His name is forever tied to the 'hearts and minds' approach to beating the insurgents, which was the key to the British success in Malaya. Templer's methods, it may be argued, expressed British liberal values in war, and 'hearts and minds' best articulated the British army's ethos of minimum force and concern for civilians. For this Britain could be justifiably proud of its campaign in Malaya. This, however, is part fact, part victor's narrative.

Against the backdrop of Malaya, it is useful to call up the late imperial conflicts in Kenya, Palestine and Cyprus, where military violence and coercion were frequent. And we do well to remember that the Malayan brand of counter-insurgency was dictated by some unique conditions. The physical terrain, the prosperous economy, the pro-Anglo local elite and the ethnic divides between the Malays and the immigrant communities gave the government plenty of

---

6   Renick, 'The Emergency Regulations of Malaya: Causes and Effects', p. 23.

7   Hack, 'Everyone lived in fear: Malaya and the British way of counter-insurgency', p. 671.

room for manoeuvre, and allowed the British to run a counter-insurgency that eschewed excessive reliance on the military.

This is not a new development in the chronicle of imperial wars. Even in the late Victorian period and between the two world wars, the defenders of Empire were aware of the impacts of government actions on civilian morale. In Malaya officials were too politic to make reference to the archaic term imperial policing. Nonetheless, imperial policing, with its deft mixture of military violence, 'example setting' punishment and protection of civilians set the template for operations on the ground. Templer's 'hearts and minds' was as much about milk powder, clean water and health clinics as about threat and coercion. There were in 'hearts and minds' plenty of hard-edged policies and wilful violence.

The knotty issue about imperial policing was how to use the military to do the policemen's work. Policing by regular soldiers sometimes created spectacular successes, but it faced specific problems. Imperial wars were waged against irregular troops of 'native savages' who did not follow the customary rules of warfare. As a result, 'We must adopt our principles to the nature of the enemy.' The saying came from Major-General Charles E. Callwell, author of the classic *Small Wars: Their Principles and Practices*.[8] Drawing on a century of Britain's experiences in suppressing colonial revolts, Callwell saw imperial wars as pitting the 'moral force of civilisation' against native opponents who were 'inferior' or 'semi-civilised'. He coined the term 'butcher and bolt' to describe the classic punitive raids – the burning of houses and destruction of crops and cattle – on the native villages.

Yet Callwell was not unaware of the ill effects of military raids and intimidation. Wreaking havoc upon native villagers and their families have been warranted punishment, but it was just as likely to destroy their trust and assimilation into the Empire. Nonetheless, Callwell never belittled the importance – and legitimacy – of military violence imposed on the natives. The burning of crops and killing of cattle were to produce a punishing economic effect by destroying the rebels' most valued assets. 'If the enemy cannot be touched in his patriotism or his honour', Callwell writes, 'he can be touched through his pocket.'[9] Apart from economic destruction, the point of punitive raids was to teach 'savage' tribes 'a lesson which they will not forget'. After all, Callwell writes, 'uncivilised races attribute leniency to timidity ... [They] must be thoroughly brought to book and cowed or they will rise again.'[10]

---

8   Charles Callwell, *Small Wars – Their Principles and Practice*, London: HMSO, 1898.
9   Ibid., p. 42.
10 Ibid., p. 148.

What he called 'the moral effect' of military raids became the crux of imperial policing. As the use of regular troops in 'small wars' often proved long drawn out and expensive – Callwell knew about the mud-slog of search-and-destroy missions long before Vietnam – military violence must be applied decisively and must generate maximum impact. Not only the rebels but the population too must be made to feel the effects of the regular troops, and terror and awe of the government. The principle of Callwell's 'small wars' method rested on the dual cornerstones of British imperialism: the assumption of its racial and civilizational advancement, and its superior firepower and troop deployment.

Callwell can come across as a parody of late-Victorian prejudices. By the time Major-General Sir Charles Gwynn published his *Imperial Policing*[11] in 1934, the tone had became more cautions. Gwynn showed a greater sensitivity towards the alienating effects of the military when used to restore law and order. In guerrilla warfare, he writes,

> [E]lusive rebel bands must be hunted down, and protective measures are needed to deprive them of opportunities. . . . [But] excessive severity may antagonise [the population], add to the number of the rebels, and leave a lasting feeling of resentment and bitterness.[12]

Compared with Callwell, Gwynn advocated a more 'civilian-centred' focus in counter-insurgency. Nonetheless he too put a great deal of emphasis on the 'moral effects' of government measures. 'The power and resolution of the Government forces must be displayed. Anything which can be interpreted as weakness encourages those who are sitting on the fence to keep on good terms with the rebels.'[13] He advocated the use of air power in bombing and strafing rebel villages, and he thought machine guns could be 'usefully employed without any suspicion of ruthlessness.'[14]

In Malaya Templer was forever aligned with the 'hearts and minds' approach, as if he had invented it. But for all the refinement he brought to it, the seeds had been sown by Callwell and Gwynn. Both understood the basic dilemma of imperial wars. To destroy the native antagonists and to create effects of 'awe and terror', government troops would often resort to unbridled force. However, a victory so won tended to be short-lived, as government violence

---

11 Sir Charles William Gwynn, *Imperial Policing*, London: Macmillan, 1934.

12 Ibid., p. 4.

13 Ibid., p. 8.

14 Ibid., p. 13.

was liable to destroy the loyalty of the natives. For the theorists of imperial policing, the idea of the 'moral effects' of government action was a significant corrective. It shifted the emphasis from hard, punitive enterprises to what we may call 'the psychological and cultural impact'. In Malaya the lessons were well learned. Direct military violence was important, but it must be moderated by a system of reward and inducement – to create government loyalty and make villagers betray the insurgents. Killing the insurgents was the aim, but so was creating a general condition of threat and warning among the people. The transformation of direct violence into intimidation: this may well be the nature of Templer's 'hearts and minds' policy. For the villagers, intimidation was barely visible, was less immediately felt than direct military coercion. This may have a 'with a pistol pointing at the temple' kind of dramatics, but it describes well life in the New Villages, where both social assistance and punishment constituted the daily life of residents.

If Templer's 'hearts and minds' drew inspiration from the 'softer, more humane principle' of modern counter-insurgency, it is because he knew Malaya of 1952 was not South Africa of 1899 or Waziristan of 1937. Compared with Callwell and Gwynn, he was more sensitive to the fact that politics and social grievances drove insurgency, and that the battlefield was now extended to civilians and to the media and public relations. The postwar conditions – and Templer's own personal insight – drove home the point. The result was a counter-insurgency that tied the defence of the Empire to the 'weapon' of social services and political concession.

IT WAS THE BIGGEST movement of people in Malaya's history. The principle of population resettlement was straightforward enough, but the scale of it and the number of people affected were epic. Under the Briggs Plan, rural squatters were to be moved from the jungle fringes and areas near the mines and plantations and resettled in constructed camps. The government had already considered the scheme during the early Emergency in August 1948. But Briggs, when appointed Director of Operations in April two years later, expanded the scale of resettlement. By the time Templer arrived, some 385,000 people had been corralled into 429 Resettlement Areas.[15]

Right from beginning the resettlement centres – Templer was to rename them 'New Villages' hint of a rural idyll – were built with military needs in

---

15 Kumar Ramakrishna, *Emergency Propaganda: The Winning of Malayan Hearts and Minds, 1948–1958*, London: Curzon, 2002, p. 94.

mind. Many resettlement centres were located in the original area of communist activity. With its home guards and police posts, it was an 'armed fortress' inserted in the heart of enemy territory. As the military solution gave way to the softer 'development approach', the site chosen had to be suitable for farming as well. Planning a New Village became a joint enterprise of the army, the police and the district agricultural officer. The favourite site was on flat land, far from surrounding hills which could serve as observation points for the enemy, and close to a river or stream to ensure a water supply to farms.[16] Resettlement, in the government's view, created a 'laboratory' for the application of 'hearts and minds'. A New Village was to be infused with bureaucratic rationality and official intent, its very logic the expression of government goodwill and benevolence. Providing security and social assistance, resettlement held the key to 'hearts and minds' as a way of winning over the villagers. Such is the Templer legend that not a few commentators look up to him as the father of the civilian-focused, humanistic brand of counter-insurgency. Michael Cohen has called this 'the myth of a kinder, gentler war' where military violence is dismissed as an embarrassment.[17] The core idea of modern counter-insurgency is to 'convince the population that counter-insurgents, acting on behalf of a sovereign government, can be trusted and are worthy of popular support'.[18] Yet, of course, military operations also 'convince' similarly. Their ferocity and 'example-setting' effects traumatize the people and shape their responses. In Malaya, if military action seemed to take second place, it was because the fight against the communists was a battle of the broadest strokes, including measures most crucial and morally insipid – the making of meaning and propaganda.

ONE OF TEMPLER'S FIRST tasks was to strengthen what Briggs had achieved. In the War Council, both military and civilian powers now came under his personal authority. He ordered the retaining of the Malayan Home Guards, whose strength lay in their numbers – reaching 250,000 in 1952, two years before he left – rather than in their ferocity or armoury. On another front, the Psychological Warfare Section dropped off leaflets – the figure was to reach 77 million in

---

16 See Sandhu, 'The saga of the "squatter" in Malaya', p. 161. Also Hamzah-Sendut, 'Planning resettlement villages in Malaya', *Journal of Environmental Planning and Management* 1(1–2), 1966, p. 60–61.

17 Michael A. Cohen, 'The Myth of a Kinder, Gentler War', *World Policy Journal* 27(1), 2010, pp. 75–86.

18 Ibid., p. 75.

Leaflet dropped on Malayan insurgents in 1953, urging them to come forward with a Bren gun and receive a $1,000 reward. (Source: U.K. Department of Information, courtesy Wikipedia Commons.)

1953 – over the jungle to induce insurgents to surrender, and used loudspeaker aircraft to broadcast messages of rewards for those who would lay down their arms and surrender.[19] The Malayan Film Unit shifted its focus from the 'increasing food production' and 'racial harmony' of the early years to news of winning the Emergency. You can still watch the films on YouTube today: after the logo of the leaping tiger, the newsreel of Templer cutting a ribbon to open a school

19 Robert Jackson, *The Malayan Emergency: The Commonwealth's War, 1948–1966*. New York: Routledge, 1991, p. 110.

88

Front page of *The Straits Times*, 1 May 1952, announcing a $250,000 reward for capture of communist leader, Chin Peng. (Source: *The Straits Times*, courtesy Wikipedia.)

or a health clinic; a morning assembly of the Malayan Police readying to patrol outside a new village; a British officer inspecting his troops, then the hard trek across muddy streams under vine-stretched canopies in search of 'terrorists' . . .

Templer also beefed up intelligence gathering. The lesson was driven home that without information about the insurgents' strength and movements, patrols and ambushes were often futile. The Special Branch, in addition to police work, was now responsible for collating information from informers, double-agents and captured or surrendered communists. A system of financial rewards was in place to induce detainees to betray and help hunt down their former comrades, with the reward halved if that person were brought back dead; M$250,000 was offered for the capture of Chin Peng.[20] The turning of insurgents into informers took place in the Holding Centre on Gurney Road on the outskirts of Kuala Lumpur, tucked away in ten acres of land surrounded by a ten-foot barbed wire fence and patrolled by armed guards. Equipped with two-way mirrors and listening devices, the interrogation rooms were designed to produce isolation and maximum psychological pressure on the detainees.

---

20 Karl Hack and C.C. Chin, *Dialogue with Chin Peng: New light on the Malayan Communist Party*, p. 300.

N O T I C E

**YOU ARE LIVING IN A FOOD RESTRICTED AREA.
WITHOUT A PERMIT YOU MAY NOT TAKE OUT OF
THIS AREA ANY OF THE FOLLOWING ARTICLES IN
HOWEVER SMALL A QUANTITY.**

**PADI · RICE · RICE PRODUCTS
TINNED FOODS · FLOUR & FLOUR PRODUCTS
SUGAR · SALT · TAPIOCA · COOKING OIL
COOKED FOODS · CONCENTRATED FOODS
DRIED FISH · PAPER
ANY MATERIAL OR INSTRUMENTS USED**

Access to food in the camps was rigorously controlled to prevent it falling into the hands of the insurgents. (Source: photo still from film footage reproduced in the 2010 History Channel documentary, 'The Malayan Emergency', online at www.youtube.com/watch?v=HgUMXHsIfe8.)

On the military front, in the last months of 1951, just before Templer's arrival, the war was beginning to turn for the government. Population resettlement launched in June the previous year was making an impact, isolating the guerrillas from their supporters and denying them food and supplies. The MCP realized victory would not be won quickly. The 1951 October Resolution of the Central Politburo, a document of copious detail running to sixty pages, called for rectifying the previous policy of slashing rubber trees and destroying identity cards for the hardship it caused the people. The MNLA fighters were to withdraw to the jungle where they would regroup and increase the planting of food crops. It was a critical strategic turn for both the MCP and the government.

As Director of Operations, Templer had under him a sizeable force including, besides British troops, Gurkha battalions, soldiers from the African Rifles and armies of Fiji, Australia and New Zealand. The military gradually shifted from broad sweeps by troops on long-range patrols to using small mobile teams, staying in one area long enough to conduct searches and gather intelligence. The improvement of jungle tactics had much to do with better information on communist couriers and food-gathering parties who used a network of jungle trails. Instead of the noisy 'jungle bashing', small platoons now operated in the jungle from ten to twenty days at a time, watching, listening and waiting to make the kill.

Population resettlement, intelligence gathering and military operations; we do not normally think of them as belonging to the same terrain as 'hearts and minds'. Yet, if Templer achieved victory not by military violence, he certainly did not win it with an approach underwritten by the government's benign intentions and humane measures alone. To get a true insight into Templer's approach, the point is not to turn our eyes back to the military and the enterprise of propaganda and misinformation. Templer's 'hearts and minds', rather than relying on a choice between military force or development and welfare assistance, was a subtle blend of the two in creating coercion and persuasion. The approach had a significant practical logic: welfare service to win over civilians works best when it is backed by decisive force; just as the harshness of decisive force can be muted – softened – by gestures of government benevolence. An offspring of imperial policing, 'hearts and minds' was built on a mingling of political pressure and official largesse, military violence and development assistance.

Against this backdrop Templer's benign reputation rested chiefly on two undertakings. One was the New Villages scheme, which we will deal with in the following chapter. The other was political reform, to prepare Malaya for independence, arguably Britain's most generous gift to the Malayan people.

In planning for Malaya's political future, Britain's intention was to protect its major assets and to ensure the country would be ruled by an elite friendly to British and Western interests. Templer was aware of the antagonism among

As part of the food denial operation against communist insurgents, Australian troops and Malayan policemen thoroughly search a small car at a roadside checkpoint in Perak state, c. 1956. (Source: Australian War Memorial, HOB/56/0796/MC.)

the three main ethnic communities. Given their mutual suspicion, Templer's endeavour to create a moderate, anti-communist alliance involved strenuous efforts of intercommunal subtlety. The Malay sultans, who saw themselves as the protectors of the Malays, had to be assured that the traditional Malay prominence in the colonial polity would not be compromised. On the other hand, the Chinese and Indians, in order to secure their loyalty and immunize them against the communists' cry against anti-colonialism, would have to be granted citizenship and basic constitutional rights. The necessary balance and compromise was, to say the least, onerous. An earlier British effort, the Malayan Union scheme, had laid out similar power-sharing arrangements and the rights of immigrant communities; it foundered in the boggy ground of Malay hostility and boycotting by the sultans and leading Malay nationalists. Now, the Emergency created a new urgency. On Templer's appointment, the Secretary of State for the Colonies had directed him to introduce legislation to pave the way for self-government and eventually independence.

With his unprecedented authority, Templer would charm, cajole and bully his way into achieving the reforms he wanted. He opened up the Malayan Civil Service, long only the domain of the British and Malays, to the Chinese and Indians. He introduced the Local Councils Ordinance to give greater Malayan representation in district councils headed by British District Officers. In the political field, the jostling for official recognition created a clear winner among the Malays, in the form of the United Malays National Organization (UMNO), founded by the Malay nationalist Dato Onn bin Ja'afar in 1946 to forestall the Malayan Union scheme. The Chinese, in order to fill the void, rallied around the Malayan Chinese Association (MCA) under Tan Cheng-Lock (later Sir Cheng-Lock Tan), a Malacca-born Straits Chinese and rubber merchant, its leader since its founding in 1949. Three years earlier, in 1946, the Malayan Indian Congress (MIC) had come into being to represent the ethnic Indians.

As the Emergency war went on, it was clear that these parties had not dispersed the distrust between the Malay, Chinese and Indian communities. Quite apart from social and economic disparities between the Malays and the Chinese, there was the fact that the communist guerrillas were mostly Chinese, while the Malays, as soldiers, home guards or police, took casualties in communist attacks. Malay extremists were quick to label the conflict as a war between Malay piety and Chinese godlessness. The government wanted to side with the Malays, yet it could not alienate the Chinese. The Templer regime (1952–54) was saved from the dilemma by a UMNO–MCA rapprochement. In early 1952, UMNO and MCA formed the National Alliance coalition,

Tan Cheng-Lock, founding leader of the Malayan Chinese Association. (Source: unknown, courtesy Wikipedia.)

which MIC joined two years later, to take part in the municipal elections. Encouraged by their electoral successes, the Alliance demanded a quicker pace towards self-government by a legislature with a majority of local members. Its leaders went to London to press their demands but to no avail. On their return, the UMNO and MCA members of the Legislative Councils staged a walk-out, making impossible the business of government. The government backed down, and finally agreed to a 52 elected-member majority to 47 officially nominated members. In the July 1954 election, the Alliance Party won 51 seats, allowing it to form the government that led to independence three years later.[21] The High Commissioner may not have himself granted Malaya nationhood, but he had brought about the conditions and policies that made independence feasible. Many Malayans saw the Templer leadership

---

21 A good summary of the shifting political scene of the pre-independence years is: Victor Purcell, *Malaysia*, London: Thames and Hudson, 1965, pp. 112–120.

as one of the major factors that brought the end of the communist menace. And he did it by making nonsense of the MCP struggle for national liberation when independence was already assured.

The political reform, while it served British interests, may also be seen as a best expression of the colonial power's reasonableness and liberal values. Certainly, the promise of independence won 'hearts and minds'. As a part of the repertoire of policies and measures that made up Temple's counter-insurgency measures, it took the wind out of the sails of the MCP aim of national self-determination. It is a long way from the Victorian imperial policy, and it finds an echo today in the ideas of 'good governance', 'civic reconstruction' and so on that pepper the pages of the 2007 US Army and Marine Corps counter-insurgency manual FM 3-24.[22] Reading the manual, one is struck how 'hearts and minds' policies involve a much wider political canvas than health clinics and milk powder: a comprehensive psychological method we associate with 'changing people's minds' in wars. In Malaya, Templer's 'hearts and minds' was directed, broadly to all players in the insurgency – the average Malayans, the inmates in the resettlement centres, the insurgents and their supporters. It is a form of power and coercion written over the 'souls' of the Malayan society at large. In its application, often there is barely a difference between insurgents and civilians. Both are caught in the net of the civilian-centred counter-insurgency or COIN, as manual FM 3-24 puts it. 'Hearts and minds', like COIN, is civilian-friendly, and for the Malayan villagers its all-embracing effects were hard to escape.

IN THE ANNALS OF modern warfare, the turning point was the French Revolution. When exported to the rest of Europe, its ideas and strategies gave conflicts between nations a new social and cultural dimension. In revolutionary France, soldiers were citizen volunteers, not professionals or gang-pressed; and they fought wars with passion and social urgency. For Lazare Carnot (1753–1823), founder of the French Revolutionary Army, revolutionary war was *guerre à outrance*, 'unlimited war', an idea echoed in Karl von Clausewitz's 'absolute war'. Both signalled a new development in the art of European warfare. The change was not only technological, which explains the war's unprecedented ferocity and destructiveness, or organizational, which made possible the supplying of forces in battles across continents; it also involved what is called the 'human

---

22 *The Manual* is co-published with the University of Chicago Press, 2007, a sign of the time.

dimension of war'.[23] Under 'human dimension' we would place state ideology and policy, the political will to carry a conflict to its 'logical end', the motivating of the citizen soldiery, and national values.

'Hearts and minds' policies can be thought of as a final expression of the transformation of warfare in the mid-twentieth century. It was, and still is, a particular preoccupation of the Western liberal-democratic states: there wasn't much 'winning over the population' in Russia's actions in Chechnya or the Sri Lankan army's campaign against the Tamil Tigers. The harnessing of Western liberal values to modern counter-insurgency raises the interesting question: Why do Western states see 'hearts and minds' policies as a morally credible way of fighting insurgents? A nation's values and the character of its people are expressed through the wars it wages. Yet, national values and culture are never immune from self-deception and collective mystification. Instead of an expression of national values, war – and the way we remember it – helps to create an image we desire of ourselves. Writing from Australia, I have watched with cringing unease how every news report on the television about Australian troop activities in Afghanistan, including those of the SAS warriors, has been about stabilization and civic reconstruction. It was as if all the firepower and technology at their disposal whose functions were to kill, to maim and to destroy, were for show. Unlike during the Malayan Emergency, scenes of, destruction and the litter of the dead rarely if ever got into the newsman's camera.

However, 'hearts and minds', the humane way of fighting insurgents, could not escape moral condemnation for its use of violence and intimidation. What saved it was deft public-relations massaging, of which Templer was a master. Winning a war by 'hearts and minds' is a good story for any nation involved in an insurgency war. Winning by sheer military might and prodigious killing, if prolonged and consuming an unacceptable amounts of citizen-soldiers and money, leads to hostile public opinion and perhaps the home government's downfall.

In the end, one can't help noting the vulgar materialism in all the talk about 'winning over the population'. In Malaya, when people, like my father, put themselves behind the government, they did so with a good deal of 'what's in it for me?' practical wisdom. My father was never slavishly loyal to the Empire; he never learned English, and what stood for British culture in Malaya – the BBC, the British Council, news from London – were foreign to him. Com-

---

23 See Charles Townshends stimulating, 'People's War', in Charles Townshend (ed.), *The Oxford History of Modern War*, Oxford: Oxford University Press, 2005, pp. 177–196.

munist China had made him distrust all governments. In Malaya he watched and assessed and calculated, and finally it was *he* who decided the colonial authorities were worthy of his allegiance. Among people in the New Villages, a similar reckoning must have gone through their minds. The 'milk powder for political subservience' transaction may turn out to be much more complex than the 'hearts and minds' legend would have it.

'Hearts and minds', it always seems to me, carries some crass assumptions about human nature. For the Malayan people, to inform on the insurgents in return for cash was certainly a case of exploiting greed 'in place of civic virtue', as Emergency expert Kumar Ramakrishna suggests.[24] In Malaya, even political concession could be dangled in front of people to bait their loyalty. However, from the 'unlimited war' of the eighteenth century, to Mao's 'people's war', to the current ISIS insurgency in Syria and Iraq, human conflicts have carried a large measure of 'intangibles' – ideologies, nationalisms, cultures, religious and political aspirations. That national development brought a British victory says a good deal about many things, not only the government's facility and talent in beating the communists. One has to put oneself in the mind of, say, an Afghani villager who chooses the Taliban over the West-supported government and the International Security Assistance Force (ISAF). How paltry are the welfare services and political reform compared with the idea of a pure Islamic state free of infidel invaders. The final outcome of a counter-insurgency is explained by many things, many beyond the scope of government initiative and commitment. Historical circumstances, ideological climate, international opinion, and luck which even a Temple, or a Briggs couldn't do without, all play their part. And to these factors we must add revolutionary consciousness or the lack of it among the oppressed. In the end, 'hearts and minds' looks less and less like the magical approach that its legend describes. In Malaya Templer won through his almost religious belief in the 'weapon' of political concession, social services and development assistance. But it was also because the conditions in Malaya were right for Templer's planning to be transformed into success.

---

24 Kumar Ramakrishna, *Emergency Propaganda,* p. 117.

6 On 'Hearts and Minds' – II
New Villages and 'war by philanthropy'

If we are not going to do something fairly good for the Colonial Empire, and something which helps them to get proper social services, we shall deserve to lose the colonies and it will only be a matter of time before we get what we deserve.
– Secretary of State for the Colonies, Malcolm MacDonald (1938–40)

Control of the masses . . . is the master weapon of modern warfare.
– Roger Trinquier, *Modern Warfare: A French View of Counter-insurgency* (1964)

The language is as coldly bureaucratic as the process it describes. 'Regrouping' is distinguishable from 'resettlement', but both mean the relocation of people and their families from different locales to government-controlled centres. 'Regrouping' targeted people living on land and in dwellings provided by mines and rubber estates. These people were technically not squatters, but settlers living on half-acre blocks provided by their company-employers. Since they had contact with insurgents whose clandestine visits extracted supplies and 'donations', the Emergency measures were applied to them. Dispersed around the mines and plantations, they were moved into new, concentrated, defensible sites within the perimeters of company land.

'Regrouping' was a joint enterprise of the government and business interests. While the government decided on the suitable location and provided the troops and police for defence, all else fell on the company. It built the new huts, fitted each with sewerage and piped water, and paid for the fences and police barracks and guard posts. Helping the workers to settle in, each mine

97

or plantation ensured a certain standard of living for those living in the camps. Traditionally 'company benevolence' allowed labourers and their families to live on company land. These homesteads created a reserve of workers for the companies, which drew on them when needed, and sent them back to live on their farm plots during times of economic downturn. Regrouping now admixed improving 'the efficiency and contentment' of the labourers with the military needs of defence and isolating them from insurgents.

The process created, on company land, a series of compact, orderly built areas. Each resembled a company town, with its own stores and paved roads linking the dwellings, but with the look of a military barracks. Barbed wired fences enclosed the settled areas – the workers' huts, the offices, stores and smokehouses, engine rooms and the manager's house. About two-thirds of a million people were affected.[1]

'Resettlement', in contrast, was an entirely government affair and of more substantial scale. It was a massive movement of people never before witnessed in Malaya, and a great chunk of the countryside was transformed into villages and towns previously non-existent. 'Resettlement' was a unique, state-directed 'town planning', one larded with the logic of defence and population control. It was, in the words of E.H.G. Dobby, a British geographer at the University of Malaya in the early fifties, 'part of an elaborate "combined operation" by military and civilian personnel' to provide 'a positive and working alternative to counter the ideological argument' of the communists.[2]

Six months into the Emergency, in December 1948, the government appointed the Squatter Committee to advise on resettlement. The Committee presented a series of recommendations: that squatters living in areas that could not be protected by police would be resettled; that those in areas free from communist terrorism would be given legal licences to their land; and that any squatter who refused resettlement, if a Chinese alien, would be repatriated to China. These were adopted by the government. Given the massive undertaking, wholesale resettlement did not begin until the arrival of General Sir Harold Briggs, the first Director of Operations, in early 1950. With a long military career in the Indian Army, Briggs had also fought in East Africa and the Western Desert in Libya; he had commanded the 5th Indian Infantry Divi-

---

1 See E.H.G. Dobby, 'Resettlement transforms Malaya: A case-study of relocating the population of an Asian plural society', *Economic Development and Cultural Change* 1(3), p. 167.

2 Ibid., p. 166.

New Villages established in 1951. (Source: based on a map shown in the 2010 History Channel documentary, 'The Malayan Emergency', online at www.youtube.com/watch?v=HgUMXHsIfe8.)

sion Brigade which turned the tide of the Japanese invasion of Burma after the battle at Imphal. When he put the Briggs Plan into effect in June that year, the war was not going well for the government. At the peak of communist violence, MNLA guerrillas were attacking railways and public buses, ambushing army and police patrols, destroying rubber trees and sabotaging mine equipment. The security forces achieved an impressive number of kills, but the MNLA seemed to have no trouble finding new recruits. Many in the government

Aerial view of a newly completed government-funded resettlement village. (Source: Imperial War Museums, K 13796.)

begin to realize victory would be years rather than months away. Among the far-sighted, the thinking began to shift from pure military action to destroying the morale and support infrastructure of the insurgents. The Briggs Plan reflected the new spirit of how to run the war. Military action was important, but perhaps more so was the dispensing of government largesse in the form of social services and agricultural assistance to induce the rural Chinese to rally to the government's side. The resettlement camps or New Villages were built with these needs in mind.

The early resettlements were poorly executed, creating shanty-town-like townships and villages. E.H.G. Dobby described the New Villages as 'geometrical in form, squared in their details of road and paths'; he thought them 'monotonous and repetitious in design and makeshift in appearance – if not in intention.'[3] Using local materials, each hut had a thatch roof of palm leaf and wooden walls. To speed up the construction in areas pressed by communist infiltration, corrugated iron sheets replaced palm leaves for roofs and concrete and cement went into flooring, posts and foundations. Defence consisted of

---

3   Ibid., p. 168.

barbed wire fences, police posts and watchtowers, with floodlighting where electricity was available. Six decades on, the New Villages are now prosperous townships of houses and small factories, but you can get a sense of their original form from old aerial photographs. You can see the dotted pattern of buildings and homesteads intersected by gridlines of roads and footpaths, the formal neatness of a well-planned suburban housing estate. Squint your eyes and you can just about make out the fence line as it skirts the boundaries that enclose the assortment of buildings and workshops. Outside the fences is a spread of dredging machines and earth-coloured open mines, or a massive green of rubber trees edging towards the jungle – MNLA guerrilla country...

The removal of farmers, especially in the first years of the Emergency, was often carried out by force. It typically took place by the first light of morning without warning. The entire area was cordoned off by troops and police. Then entered the Chinese-speaking administrative officers entered, accompanied by more troops and police, followed by land officers, veterinary experts, social workers, and doctors and nurses. People were told they were to be relocated, and to bring their things and load them into the waiting lorries. Compensation for possessions left behind – the huts, the animal sheds, the fruit trees, the

Entrance to a New Village near Ipoh, Perak state, 1952. (Source: unknown, courtesy IpohWorld, www.ipohworld.org.)

High Commissioner Sir Henry Gurney (left) inspecting a New Village in Jelebu, Negri Sembilan state. (Source: unknown.)

crops still to be harvested – were calculated on the spot. In some cases, the new town or village was fairly well completed before people moved in. In others, only the perimeter and dormitory had been finished and the task of building the huts fell on the incoming dwellers.

People were often reluctant to move. A settler many years on recalls the scene: the weeping women and men in silent rage, the prevalent misery at having to leave their homesteads, the general chaos, the surrounding troops. The men and women were vacating their hearth and home, and land which in the chaotic war years had taken on a mystical sense of ownership and permanence. They had existed independently in near self-sufficiency; now in a new, strange place they found themselves living cheek by jowl with other families, and in the protective embrace of a forceful government. Old people who once lived in such camps, with some not too subtle urging from the researcher-interviewer, now speak of 'losing everything' before moving into 'a concentration camp': bitter language stemming from a sense of historical wrong that has found no redress.[4]

The New Villages were anything but concentration camps, however. For once past the guard posts and the barbed wire fences, what they found was all

---

4   For the use of the concentration camp metaphor, see Tan Ten-Phee, "'Like a Concentration Camp, lah": Chinese grassroots experience of the Emergency and new villages in British Colonial Malaya', *Chinese Southern Diaspora Studies*, 3, 2009, pp. 216–28.

government benevolence. After being screened for communist sympathizers, families were interviewed by land officers and veterinary experts. Social workers, doctors and nurses then took over, and family members were given a medical examination. Each household received a small allowance to tide them over until they could be self-sufficient on new land which they now owned, with legal title. Apart from houses and small farm plots, the most established New Villages would each have a school, a post office, a health centre and dispensary, a market place and government offices. With these provisions, Dobby writes with grave irony, '[I]t was hoped to offset the admitted nuisance and hardship [of a new life] under police and military guards.'[5]

REGROUPING AND RESETTLEMENT BROUGHT a total of almost a million people under 'government protection'. The programme had called for vast logistics. The British government, forever concerned about picking up the bills for expenses incurred by the colonies, was relieved when the Malayan government agreed it would carry most of the resettlement budget. In this Malaya's finances were bolstered by fortuitous circumstances. In 1950 with the outbreak of the Korean War global demand and US stockpiling pushed up the prices of rubber and tin, bringing unprecedented prosperity to Malaya. In that year, the resettlement programme was allocated the amount of M$7 million. Of this, M$3.8 million was spent on housing grants, subsidies and family allowances. The remaining M$3.2 million enabled the government to buy land and construct roads, drainage, latrines, community halls, police posts, and wire fences. (The 1950 budget placed an order for 2,156 tons of barbed wire.)[6] By the end of 1951, the second year of the programme, the budget had increased almost six-fold to M$41 million. The 1950–2 Government Development Plan provided the breakdown: the bulk for housing grant, subsistence allowance, preparation of site, fencing and so on, M$29.89 million; for police buildings, M$6.39 million; M$2.38 million for land acquisition; and the rest for schools, health services and agricultural aid. At the end of June 1953, a total of 546 New Villages had been built and 570,838 people were settled.[7] That year the rubber price inflated by the Korean War boom collapsed; but by then the resettlement had been virtually completed.

---

5   E.H.G. Dobby, 'Resettlement transforms Malaya', p. 169.

6   Renick, 'The Emergency Regulations of Malaya: Causes and Effects', p. 11.

7   Ibid., p. 25.

Historian Karl Hack calls the period 1950–52 a "'clear and hold" state of the counter-insurgency'.[8] The population control, involving as it did the spatial confinement of villagers, broke the back of the insurgents. Food control and the denial of comfort and support to the MNLA were working. Towards the end of 1951, the MCP set about to break up the guerrilla bands into smaller units, reassign fighters to jungle planting, and reduce the sabotage and assassinations that had hurt mostly civilians. The aim was to win back civilian support, as well as to give a greater focus to subversion and infiltration. The MCP October 1951 Directive that outlined the strategic retreat was evidence of the devastating effects of population relocation.[9]

Overall the British success was aided by several factors. The hike of rubber and tin prices was one. The other was Britain's determination to carry the Emergency to the end at a time when it was scaling down colonial wars and withdrawing from its overseas territories. At the height of the Emergency, in 1952, to move against less than 8,000 insurgents, Britain deployed 40,000 British and Commonwealth troops, 60,000 police and 250,000 Home Guards.[10] Britain's military and political commitment, the size of the security forces, lukewarm public response at home to a distant war, and MCP's tactical miscalculations – this explains of the 'effectiveness' of the New Villages in the minds of Templer's admirers.

Yet, the story of the New Villages is less attractive when we remember the unsavoury counter-insurgency measures that gave birth to them. Population relocation had other names in other imperial wars: Lord Kitchener's 'depopulation' of the South African veld during the Second Boer War (1899–1902), the American military's 'population reconcentration' in the Philippine Insurrection (1899–1902), France's *regroupement* that removed nearly two million people from their villages during the Algerian War of Independence (1954–62). These measures shared the broad, common aim of scuttling the cosy relationship between the guerrillas and the villagers whose grievances fuelled the rural struggle. As Alistair Horne describes in his classic, *A Savage War of Peace: Algeria 1954–1962*, *regroupement* produced a land denuded of people,

---

8   Karl Hack, 'Everyone lived in fear: Malaya and the British way of counter-insurgency', *Small Wars & Insurgencies* 23(4–5), 2012, p. 673. Hack is one of the more astute writers on the Emergency, who has much to say on the government counter-terror of 1948–49.

9   Karl Hack and C.C. Chin, *Dialogue with Chin Peng: New light on the Malayan Communist Party*, 144–70.

10 Hack, 'Everyone lived in fear', p. 4.

crops and general signs of life. Once transferred to the resettlement camps, the villagers lived a torpid existence under the shadow of surveillance and threat of violence.[11] To the contemporary mind, the features of the resettlement camps have become all too familiar: barbed wire fences and watchtowers, accommodation huts and makeshift amenities, armed guards patrolling the camp and keeping an eye on the listless inmates in confinement – the nightmare vision of a concentration camp.

In Malaya population resettlement never fell into such disrepute. In the Emergency fable resettlement had worked, its measures untinged by the morally repugnant. The New Villages were a good story of the Emergency, and we applaud the British genius of making resettlement the cornerstone of the conflict. Yet population relocation has also been, in modern times, a social and moral disaster. The strategic hamlet programme, a brainchild of Robert Thompson, who once served under Briggs and Templer, made no difference to the Vietnam War's final end. In French Algeria, the brutal repression of which civilian *regroupement* was symbolic eventually caused the fall of the French Fourth Republic (1946–58), a French army mutiny, and ultimately the French withdrawal from the North African colony.

TO UNDERSTAND THE SUCCESS of population relocation in Malaya, we need to sketch a wide arc of causes and circumstances. We must also give heed to resettlement's particular spatial logic and why it worked. The concept and design of a New Village demands much probing. If it was not a concentration camp, it certainly took on the features of a prison or any place of incarceration or detention. However, it can be said that a New Village was more like a hospital or an old-age home, a benign institution of confinement. Prisons are not hospitals or old-age homes, but they all share the bureaucratic aims of order and discipline. A system of rules and regulations mark out each place from the ordinary world, and the life of the inmates from the sunny realm outside. Prisons and hospitals, as much as the New Villages, make for what the sociologist Erving Goffman calls 'total institutions.'[12]

We need something like the concept of 'total institution' to show up the moral morbidity of the Malayan resettlement scheme. Goffman is speaking of

---

11 Alistair Horne, *A Savage War of Peace: Algeria 1954–1962*, New York: New York Review of Books, 2006, pp. 220–1.

12 Erving Goffman, *Asylums: Essays on the social situation of mental patients and other inmates*, New York: Anchor Books, 1961.

the more charitable institutions, but he might as well be describing the New Villages. As with other 'total institutions', the myriad of restrictions that ruled the lives of those inside were 'for their own good.' In Goffman's language, the New Villages restored the squatter-farmers to their duties of good citizenry. As with a hospital or a prison, population resettlement is a socially rehabilitative undertaking. The harsh discipline and restrictions worked to 'heal' the moral frailty of villagers all too often choosing fence-sitting than supporting the government. At the core of it, what drives any 'total institution' is the pervasive, often baroque regime of disciplinary rules and directives. (Goffman makes much of the significance of uniforms, such as the proverbial white coat that signals the power and authority of the medical staff.) A prison's rules are punitively harsh and designed to be so, but those of a hospital or an old-age home carry tender-hearted and sympathetic meanings, and patients more or less submit to them voluntarily. However, as with the New Villages, benevolence is the other side of the rules and restrictions of a caring institution. If inmates cannot escape the monitoring regulations, neither can they avoid the solicitude, the doting custodianship. Both are equally hard to break free from.

The 'total' of the 'total institution' is really about the pervasiveness, the comprehensiveness, of the bureaucratic order that carves a place out of the ordinary world. Ask any long-term patient: a hospital can be a setting of power and subservience. As for the New Villages, the armed guards and barbed wire fences were not the only means of control and coercion. The delivery of official largess also served to enforce compliance especially when, as it often happened, such largess was deemed a privilege for the worthy, to be withdrawn at will by the government. All this is unhappy talk in the official narrative. A New Village bolstered bureaucratic efficiency. It corralled people into a concentrated space where government could try out the policies and initiatives of a new era. As a counter-insurgency measure, a resettlement centre became a place of propaganda and mystification: inside the bubble of government protection another kind of war could be waged.

WHEN THE BRIGGS PLAN was put in place, one of its aims called for civic education and for the giving to people a direct experience of self-government. The District Office appointed members of the village committee that ran a New Village's daily affairs under the guidance of the Resettlement Officer, usually a Chinese-speaking British civil servant. Later, in early 1953, Templer's 'self-government from the ground up' brought elections to the New Villages and people elected their own members to the committee. To give substance to

Squatter resettlement under the Briggs Plan, 1950. The inaugural meeting of a co-operative society formed by Chinese civilians resettled in a New Village. With them are officials from the Federal Department of Co-operative Societies, welfare workers and police officers, 1950. (Source: Imperial War Museums, GOV 3821)

local government, the village committee was later given the authority to raise taxes. Villagers learned a good deal from the experience. The local elections eventually encouraged people to register and take part in the first Federation Legislative Council election when it was held in 1955.[13]

However, these exercises were not the unifying, patriotic affair the government had in mind. Nation-building on the craggy ground of ethnic mutual distrust was not to be easy. Among other things, touching on population resettlement was the perennial issue of land. Resettlement needed land for building houses and for farming. However, land was, and still is today, one of the special rights of Malays in the form of Malay Reserve Land. By law, land gazetted Malay Reserve Land may not be 'sold, leased, or otherwise disposed of except to a Malay', a measure to protect Malay ownership from that of non-Malays, especially the Chinese. All the same, the Emergency and the communist threat forced the sultans to moderate their positions. Under government pressure, they gave up some of the gazetted Malay Reserve Land, though this was done

---

13 See Salma Nasution Khoo and Abdur-Razzaq Lubis, *Kinta Valley: Pioneering Malaysia's Modern Development*, Ipoh, Malaysia: Perak Academy, 2011, p. 315.

mostly in the form of land grants rather than by their wholesale alienation to non-Malays. Resettlement had produced one of the first major concessions by the Malay elite to the non-Malays.[14]

By the time of Templer's arrival, self-government and eventual independence had become the rallying cry of the 'hearts and minds', providing an incentive for Malayans to support the fight against communists. Land reform was for the Chinese an opportunity to jostle for a bigger part in this national development. The Malayan Chinese Association (MCA), founded in 1949, saw its main mission as the fostering of Chinese interests and rebutting the charge of disloyalty. The fact that the communist insurrection was largely a Chinese undertaking weighed heavily on the MCA. Throughout the resettlement processes, the MCA helped with smoothing communal relations and lent support to the government. It encouraged the Chinese to join the Home Guard, it actively assisted information and intelligence gathering, it raised funds through lotteries and donations to assist welfare projects in the New Villages. Resettlement was a crucial training ground for the MCA. Through the Emergency the Chinese had to learn the subtle art of how to present themselves as loyal government subjects, unlike their fellow ethnics in the jungle. More important perhaps, the village committee elections helped the MCA to work out a mode of electoral politics that it still practises today – a mixture of 'big man politics', the use of wealth and patronage, and sidling up to the UMNO in the formation of political coalition.

Elections, you might say, helped to foster a feeling among Malayans of being stakeholders in a rapidly evolving political scene. They spoke of government concession, of official willingness to listen to the people in the shaping of their political future. Meanwhile, in the New Villages, the Emergency fomented another reality, as its regulations and violence bore down hard on the settlers. Even Briggs or Templer would have admitted it was something of a Faustian bargain that went on. The health clinics and schools and farm assistance improved people's lives. Yet, if these gestures of official largess won their loyalty, it also allowed the government to apply a particular form of *threat*, of intimidation, to the recipients.

This begins to make sense when we recognize the government grants and assistance as what they were: a key instrument in the power play of 'hearts and minds'. For the villagers, as their eyes glowed over the government's generosity, would also watch nervously the ever-present restrictions that applied to

14 R. D. Renick, 'The Emergency Regulations of Malaya: Causes and Effects', pp. 4–5.

their daily activities in the camp. If official benevolence was a fact, so were the curfews, the search at the gate each morning as people left for work outside, the raids of homes suspected of harbouring insurgents or Min Yuen agents. Even the more docile among the villagers would recognize this: the gifts of government were no free lunch, they had to be paid for, not the least by one's freedom and submission. The authorities understood that the armed guards and midnight raids killed insurgents as much as they threatened and intimated their supporters in the New Village. But threat and intimidation could also be achieved when the government would, at the right moment, withdraw or deny the privileges, the signs of official goodwill.

Drawing on imperial policing, Templer's 'hearts and minds' policy was about neither official benevolence nor coercion, but a subtle mixture of the two. In the New Villages, food control, curfew and restriction of movement hit people the hardest; for them the relaxation of these impediments was the most appealing. When it happened, it restored some degree of normalcy to daily life, and people's dignity seemed less compromised. However, this was often the case of 'the hand that giveth, that hand taketh it away'. Once some measure of freedom had been granted, the government could, as a deliberate measure, easily change its mind – to give warning, to show the tough hand of officialdom, and to teach people a lesson. One of the areas where this was strategically applied was collective punishment.

TANJONG MALIM IS A rubber estate town in Selangor state, surrounded by several New Villages at an 18-mile radius. In March 1952, a communist ambush took place on the outskirts and killed twelve people – ten policemen, a Public Works engineer and the 32-year-old Michael Codner, the Assistant District Officer. Codner, a war hero whose escape from a German POW camp was recounted in the film, *The Wooden Horse*, died on his way to repair a water pipeline in a rubber estate. After the incident, the police sought information from the people, but no one came forward. Three days later, a furious Templer arrived and cursed and harangued the people for their complicit silence. He imposed a twenty-two-hour daily curfew on the 20,000 residents. He reduced the food ration, closed the schools, and stopped the buses and rickshaws from running; people were only allowed to leave their homes from noon to two in the afternoon. The curfew created a dead town; even pawnshops soon closed after running out of cash as out-of-work town folks rushed to pawn their valuables.

A week later, in what came to be called 'the Tanjong Malim technique of obtaining information', a letter enclosing a questionnaire was delivered to each

A government demand for information – 'the Tanjong Malim technique'. (Source: photo still from the 2010 History Channel documentary, 'The Malayan Emergency', online at www.youtube.com/watch?v=HgUMXHsIfe8.)

household. The head of the family was to give any information he or she knew, and name the communists and their sympathisers, or he or she could leave the form blank. The forms were then collected, put in a sealed metal box and sent directly to King's House, Templer's official residence. There, in a ritual befitting of the colourful man, the High Commissioner, under the watchful eyes of the community leaders, opened the box, read each letter and jotted down the answer if any, before having them taken out to be destroyed. To the company present, he barked, 'Go back and tell them how their letters were brought straight to me.' Only then were the community leaders allowed to journey back to Tanjong Malim. Templer ordered lifting the collective punishment after he found the information he needed in the letters.[15]

Three months later, in August, a similar punishment was meted out to the small village of Permatang Tinggi. There, a Chinese resettlement officer was shot dead in a coffee shop in the presence of a dozen people. In the police questioning, no one admitted having seen what happened. The sixty-two villagers of Permatang Tinggi already had a bad reputation for supporting the communists and two Chinese civilians had been killed since February. On 22 August, a Thursday, Templer arrived in an armoured car. He gathered the villagers together and uttered this threat and warning:

---

15 Barber, *The War of the Running Dogs*, pp. 142–3.

None of you will leave your houses. If you want food you can ask a police-man to get it for you. If by next Monday you have not given the informa-tion in your possession I shall apply Emergency Regulation 17D to every inhabitant of this village. .... Maintain your silence and you will go into detention – everyone, man, woman and child. If you co-operate, but are afraid of communist vengeance, we will resettle you elsewhere.

And he reminded them:

Your village is surrounded. A wire fence has been put around it and no one will be allowed to escape. Does anyone want to ask me any questions? No questions? All right, 9 a.m. on Monday, then.

The Permatang Tinggi folk turned out to be a much tougher lot than those in Tanjong Malim. No one talked, no one filled in the questionnaire issued to each household; the 'Tanjong Malim technique' did not work. On the follow-ing Monday, true to his word, Templer had the villagers taken to a detention centre and ordered their houses and shops to be demolished. A year later most of the detainees were released; only half of them volunteered to move to a New Village constructed nearby; the rest chose the banal martyrdom of returning to Permatang Tinggi. Lulled by their lucky escape, the villagers could even indulge in a bit of black humour. Pointing to an old man said to be the only one who told the truth, they joked: 'He didn't hear a thing, he's stone deaf.'[16]

In March 1953, the following year, Templer announced in the Legislative Council the repeal of Emergency Regulation 17D. Collective punishment was legally off the books. Nonetheless Templer continued with his method of wily manipulation. He was fond of dropping in on a village without warning. After he had meted out punishment to the Permatang Tinggi folks, on the same day he had proceeded to another village a short distance away. Here he was all sweetness and charm, as he told the villagers:

We want to finish with all this nonsense. We want to make New Villages like this happy place. (We want to finish this so-called Emergency, so that we can spend money on providing the New Villages and the Malay Kampongs with proper water and light and all the other amenities of decent living. We cannot do it with this Emergency on because the Government's money is all spent on the Emergency. You people can help us to finish it. Good luck to you all.[17]

---

16 Cloake, *Templer, Tiger of Malaya: the life of field marshal Sir Gerald Templer*, pp. 272–3.
17 Ibid., p. 274.

In September 1953, he declared a new chapter in the effort to win 'hearts and minds'. He declared some 200 square miles of Malacca state a 'white area'. There, the customary food control, night curfew, and restrictions on the movement of goods and people were lifted.[18] Everyone thought that this was the prelude to the ending of the Emergency.

For the government, the new declaration was meant to garner significant propaganda value. A 'white area' was to be a major step forward, an area free of communist activities, a reward for those willing to give information and cooperate with the government. It demonstrated that the fight against the communists was bearing fruit, and how government successes would quickly translate into direct benefits for the villagers. Compared with collective punishment, a 'white area' was all affirmation and encouragement. A 'white area' is not a 'free area', however. The New Villages so classified were still a place of strong government and police presence. Jungle squads still patrolled and laid ambush outside the camps, people could not move out to live elsewhere, and they had to help with defence and maintaining the Home Guard. People were expected to report on any resurgence of communist activities, and police and troops continued to search the farmers and workers leaving the gate each morning. The 'white New Villages' may have been free from many restrictions, but the Emergency Regulations continued to apply.

Templer left Malaya in mid-1954; by that time, along the coast, some 1,300,000 people in New Villages and towns were living in 'white areas'.[19] The relaxing of restrictions sometimes led to communist infiltration, as it made it easier for the Min Yuen agents to move from one New Village to another to extract money and information. But in the government's view 'the psychological advantage outweighed the risk'.[20]

CONSIDERING ITS DUBIOUS REALITY, population resettlement in Malaya has enjoyed a strangely benign reputation. One needs not go the way of the concentration camp metaphor, but one needs to remember that the New Villages' primary function was confinement, and the control and monitoring of people's activities inside them. One can make too much by Templer's bluff charisma and enthusiasm. But one must remember his 'hands-on' approach to development: his tours of the

---

18 Richard Clutterbuck, *The Long Long War: The Emergency in Malaya, 1948–1960*, London: Cassell, 1966, pp. 113, 129–31.

19 Ibid., p. 130.

20 Ibid.

New Villages, bristling with optimism; his call for more health clinics and Women's Institutes; his request to the College of Propaganda in Rome for teams of monks and nuns with experience of China.[21] Ultimately, however, these theatrics and grand gestures muted but did not soften what were, in truth, war measures.

Templer's personality and policies were things of their time. During the Cold War, the West was preoccupied with how to fight communism. In the Third World, many argued, the best way to destroy communism's appeal was social and economic development. Development promised to uplift the lives of the poor and the disenfranchised by orderly government planning and as-sistance. The idea was to blunt communism's argument for being the only way for the Third World to be free from political repression and economic impov-erishment. The approach was given the clearest expression by W.W. Rostow's *The Stages of Economic Growth,* which carried the subtitle *A Non-Communist Manifesto.*[22] Published in 1960, it put forward a formula for economic growth that captured the concerns of the liberal political thinkers of the time. If a secure livelihood and economy were communism's major appeal, Rostow argues, then the West must help to deliver them, albeit in its own political and ideological terms, leaving the status quo of the states in the underdeveloped world more or less intact. Instead of revolution, development – and modernization – were the stairways to the heaven of democracy, freedom and prosperity, with a little help from the free market. The process was to be orderly and peaceful guiding the growth of a vibrant, accumulative capitalist economy.

As an anti-communist strategy, development was also, in the widest sense, national development. In this argument, market freedom easily translates into political freedom. It is easy to see the special significance of all this in the Malayan counter-insurgency. Here development was a weapon in a 'bread and butter' war, but even government planners realized that the fight against communism could not be waged in the economic sphere alone. As prosper-ity brought loyalty to and support for the government, state planning would introduce measures that aimed to inculcate liberal, democratic values among the people. Much of counter-insurgency was about making citizens loyal, something Templer recognized clearly.

Reading about his doings and passions, one feels that Templer's thinking pre-dated Rostow's. What was 'hearts and minds' except the idea that state-directed

---

21 T.N. Harper, *The End of Empire and the Making of Malaya,* p. 185.

22 W.W. Rostow, *The Stages* of Economic *Growth: A Non-Communist Manifesto,* Cam-bridge: Cambridge University Press, 1960.

development – all those civic centres and health clinics and the agricultural assistance – must be harnessed to the desired political and military aims? What Malaya amply demonstrated was that development and political reform, when combined with substantial military force, contributed to the British success in the Emergency. For the British, what was crucial was what development meant for the villagers, and how it was tied to the government's aims and agendas. What took place inside the New Villages were measures for life's betterment for everyone. Even collective punishment was about the improvement of peace and security so that development could be carried out. For many villagers, development aims lightened the harness of government restrictions and made them liveable. If crimes were carried out in the New Villages they were 'logical crimes', crimes that had become 'theoretically defensible', in Camus' phrase. For all the violence and the punishment, counter-insurgency had government benevolence sealed on its face, as it appeared 'reasonable' and 'seek[ing] refuge in a doctrine'.[23]

In the ancient days, Camus points out, wars seemed simpler in their aims and moral claims. He writes in *The Rebel*,

> [W]hen the tyrant razed cities for his own greater glory, when the slave chained to the conqueror's chariot was dragged through the rejoicing streets, when enemies were thrown to the wild beasts in front of the assembled people, the mind did not reel before such unabashed crimes, and the judgment remained unclouded.[24]

Modern conflicts lacked such clarity, their means and ends refused easy discernment. Both the Western liberal states and the totalitarian regimes embroidered, on the flags of their marching armies the slogans of 'freedom', 'liberation', 'justice', 'historical destiny'. Both had their own population resettlement, raze-the-earth policies and collective punishment. Camus did not cast the blame only on the totalitarian regimes. Wars waged by the liberal-democratic states could be similarly savage. What stood out, though, was the way such wars were aligned with the humanitarian values they alone cherished and upheld:

> But slave camps under the flag of freedom, massacres justified by philanthropy or by a taste for the superhuman, in one sense cripple judgment. On the day when crime dons the apparel of innocence – through a curious

23 Albert Camus, *The Rebel*, London: Penguin Books, 1971, p. 11.
24 Ibid., pp. 11–12.

transposition peculiar to our times – it is innocence that is called upon to justify itself'.[25]

We condemn wars launched by the ideology of the superman; but those fought in the name of democracy and peace cannot be similarly condemned. The Malayan Emergency was not the German Wehrmacht's anti-partisan operations in Russia during the Second World War. The degrees of military violence, and the nature of their moral offences, are different. However, for Camus as for us, our judgement on the actions of the liberal democratic state is often befuddled by its alleged humanitarianism and good will. A democratic state excels in waging a 'war by philanthropy'. Since 'justice' and 'freedom' – to which we should add 'human rights' – are claimed as preoccupations of the West, we must not allow our moral assessments of its war measures and conduct to be crippled. 'Slave camps under the flag of freedom' must not be blind to our eyes.

25 Ibid., p. 12.

7 On The Malayan Left
The MCP and the 'National Question'

Pertama, saya orang Melayu. Bermula di KMM [Kesatuan Melayu Muda, Young Malays Union]. Kemudian Parti Kmunis. (I am a Malay first. I started at the KMM. Then the Communist Party.)
– CD Abdullah, General Secretary, Malayan Communist Party (2013–)[1]

In many ways, the Emergency ... was an essentially Chinese affair: a Chinese communist party, Chinese guerrillas, Chinese support – and Chinese victims.
– Anthony Short, 'Communism, race and politics in Malaysia' (1970)

Born in 1923 in a village near Parit town in Perak State, CD Abdullah, the ex-chairman of the MCP, was the most senior Malay leader of the Malayan communist movement. At his birth, the astrologer on reading his chart said he would have a short life or, if he survived, would 'cause a big problem'. CD Abdullah has obviously survived. Now in his eighties, he lives in retirement in southern Thailand, like his ex-comrades, an abject figure of history marooned in the contemporary age. As for the 'big problem' he caused, it is lodged in the nation's past, a 'foreign country' where, so it seems, only academic specialists visit. But the wheel of fate has turned in other ways for CD Abdullah. When a young boy, as he tells it in his memoirs,[2] his life was nearly cut short by a couple of freak accidents. Once, accompanying his mother

---

1 Abdullah's real name is Cik Dat bin Anjang Abdullah. He is commonly known as CD Abdullah, the name appears in the title of his *Memoirs*. He was appointed Chairman of the MCP in August 1988; he became General Secretary after Chin Peng's death in 2013.

2 *Memoirs of CD Abdullah, Part one: The movement until 1948*, Petaling Jaya, Malaysia: SIRD, 2009.

to gather snails by the river, he fell in and was swept away by the current. His mother looked everywhere for him and saw him struggling in the middle of the swirling water. Undaunted by her own lack of watery skill, she leaped in and made towards the boy, herself almost drowning. Some people witnessing the accident raced back to their village. Help finally came and retrieved mother and son from the river.

His life again hung by a thread a few years later. Then seven years old, he would row a sampan to his teacher's house every day after school to do his homework and soak up the old man's moral and religious lessons, with a dash of the heroic history of Malay resistance to colonial rule thrown in. One day was wet with light rain. When the sampan reached mid-river the current turned turbulent and threw the vessel out of control. It capsized and tossed him into the water. Clinging on to the flimsy boat, he tried to calm his panic in the raging river – there were no mother and bystanders to rescue him this time. He let loose a phrase that frequently garnished the old teacher's sermons: 'I am a son of Perak! I am a son of Perak!' The words bolstered his spirit and determination. His hand gripped the capsized sampan, and holding on for dear life he treaded the muddy water until he reached the bank safely.[3]

'I am a son of Perak! I am a son of Perak!' Was this a magical incantation from the book of geomancy, the *Tajul Muluk,* that his teacher had him learn during his visits? Was it the astrologer's charm given to him at his birth, to be called up in a life-threatening situation? It was none of these; it was only history. In the nineteenth century, resentful of the Treaty of Pangkor (1874) that installed a British Resident in the Malay court and made Perak State a British protectorate, the Malay chiefs had rebelled, leading to the assassination of the first Resident, James Birch. 'A son of Perak' reaped a fervour from the event, a fervour that would have stirred the consciousness of any Malay nationalist. CD Abdullah was only an innocent seven-year-old, yet the Perak Rebellion worked on him and calmed his panic as he clung on to the sampan. But then it could just be a legend an old man recounted to keep nostalgia and regret at bay. Whatever it was, 'son of Perak' was a potent phrase that awakened the political consciousness of a seven-year-old. Affecting and with a touch of melodrama, it is a good story to tell about the early life of a career revolutionary.

Nevertheless, magical incantation or charm is not far off. History, in the Marxist-communist scheme of things, is the enchanter's map that charts a revolution's stormy voyage from subjection to power. A revolution, when it has

---

3   Ibid., p. 6.

finally succeeded, looks back at its shaky beginnings with a sense of wonder. Slogans – 'Proletarians of all nations, unite!', 'Revolution is not a dinner party', 'Communism needs democracy like the human body needs oxygen' – cut through petty bourgeois reserve and cry out the passion, the commitments and the sacrifices communism demands of its followers. The young CD Abdullah was still many years away from communism. But the instinct for slogans so crucial for any revolutionary was already deep in him. Near death, he had called up this catchphrase so full of historical resonance. As a lifesaver, it had proved more efficacious than 'Help! Help!' or 'Save me!'

COLONIAL MALAYA IS A good example of the 'plural society' as put forward by the British historian J.S. Furnivall.[4] After joining the Indian Civil Service in 1901, he spent many years in Burma where he was Assistant Commissioner and Settlement Officer. His classic Colonial Policy and Practice, drawing on his experience as a British colonial civil servant, sounds a melancholy note. In a colonial society, he observes, the colonists, the indigenous people and the immigrant communities are all set apart from each other by language, culture, religion and custom. They live more or less separately, and meet and interact in the market place, and in the limited sphere of the colonial polity. This 'plural society' exhibits no 'normative consensus' but is internally divided under the single authority of the colonial power. It is a society without cohesion and a common will; 'the groups are held together by the market place'.[5] A plural society, Furnivall argues, is precarious and inherently unstable.

Furnivall tends to make too much of the actual dividedness of communities that make up colonial society; but he is spot on about their antagonism and conflicting social-economic interests. In Malaya the ethnic cleavages were carefully nurtured by the colonial state, helping to bolster the 'us against them' ethos central to the workings of 'divide and rule'. When Malaya gained independence in 1957, the colonial system of ethnic preference for one community – the Malays – was transferred almost wholesale to the new nation. It wreaked havoc on the constitutional arrangement that formally gave equal rights and cultural recognition to all. The result, we might say, was several 'nations' in one nation-state. In Malaysia today, our daily life is a complex negotiation through the web of ethnicism both inherited and recreated anew. The 'special privileges'

4   J.S. Furnivall, Colonial Policy and Practice: a Comparative Study of Burma and Netherlands India, Cambridge: Cambridge University Press, 1948.

5   Ibid., p. 303.

of Malays as *bumiputeras* – the original 'sons of the soil'; the sanctity of the Malay rulers and Islam; the structural divide between Malay political power and Chinese economic dominance; the heated debate about how to close the social and economic breaches between communities: all of these continue to fire up the crude debate about who owns the country and who are 'strangers' living in a country in which they do not belong. One may regret this blot on the fair escutcheon of national integration, but few can deny it.

Not surprisingly, communal allegiances also enter the story of the Malayan left. For the social groups and organized interests that made up the left, ethnicity divided them, and dictated their leadership and how to build their support. The Malay and Chinese radicals sometimes formed an alliance, but more commonly both relied on their own community for support and the recruitment of followers. Like much of Malayan social life, the 'cultural division of labour' infected progressive political circles, even the communist movement.

The Malayan–Chinese left, we recall, had come out of the struggle in the homeland for 'national survival' in the face of nineteenth-century Western imperial incursion and later the Sino–Japanese War (1937–45). Added to these are local forces in Malaya. Since the late 1800s, the mass intake of Chinese immigrant labourers to Malaya had created a community with a substantial underclass. Under the colonial policy the Chinese were left very much to themselves. In any case, Chinese self-help would help the colonial budget because the community showed such talent for funding and running their own schools and hospitals and old-age homes. Still, the authorities could not for long leave the Chinese entirely to themselves when, invariably, the struggles and political agitations in China began to spill over to the colony. This is was part of the incentive for a change to a more active official intervention in Chinese affairs, beginning with establishing the Chinese Protectorate in the Strait Settlements – Singapore, Malacca and Penang – in 1877. For the Chinese elite, this turned out to be something of a mixed blessing. While the intervention made the powerful and the wealthy the official conduit to the Chinese world, it could not but open up the morass of oppression and corruption *within*, a wound the community leaders were complicit in inflicting. In the following decades, it was clear, at least to some, that the problems of the needy and the destitute could not be left to philanthropy or the government. This was as much a matter of practicality as it was of political consciousness. The notion of 'Chinese communal interests' and their protection began to change and came to be aligned with the anti-colonial struggle.

IT IS EASY TO see how, in colonial Malaya, the protection of Chinese interests would affect other communities too. Ethnicity is a reactive affair. Each community's perceptions and understanding never stay within their borders. As people look across the fence, what happens to them – their deprivation, their powerlessness, the impediments to their better future – are the doings of others. This mutual assessment is as likely to be fired up by real socio-economic differences as it is by the fantasy and resentment. In any case, primed by this principle, when the Chinese turned more assertive of their rights and interests, they found themselves impinging on other communities, principally the Malays. The first lesson of the politics of ethnicity was learned: the Chinese left could not advance the interests of its own people without encroaching on those of the Malays.

British 'indirect rule' had traditionally relied on wealthy merchants, clan leaders, and heads of secret societies for its connections with the Chinese.[6] The anti-Qing revolution, and later the Sino–Japanese War and the Chinese civil war, each in its own way, shook up the cosy world of colonialism and Chinese compradors. In rallying for changes, radicals fixed their eyes on the colony, ready to build support among the ethnic Chinese and take on local grievances. Politically, they had learned a great deal in mobilizing aid for the ancestral land in crises; these skills were now transferred to the struggle in Malaya. Among the Chinese, a political movement would need to 'patriotic' in relation to what happened in China, while it fashioned a realpolitik for the problems facing the Chinese in Malaya.

The tensions in the Malayan–Chinese left illustrate the wider implications of Furnival's 'plural society'. Activists in any ethnic community, might well ask the question: 'A political movement demands organization and resources, sometimes our blood, so why shouldn't it be devoted to the advancement of "our people" alone? After all, it is "our people" who have sustained us, and provided the very reason for the struggle.' What resulted was the strange affliction that shaped the Chinese and the Malay left: it made them lean towards a communally obsessive 'socialism for *my people*', and 'revolution to improve of the lot of *my people*'.

The Emergency tended to produce an 'us versus them' polarity of its own. In the war against the insurgents, the line was crudely drawn: on one side, the

---

6   See Victor Purcell's classic work, *The Chinese in Malaya*, Kuala Lumpur: Oxford University Press, 1967. Purcell, a former Protector of Chinese Malaya, was a critic of the government during the Emergency for being anti-Chinese; see his *Malaya, Communist or free*, Stanford: Stanford University Press, 1955.

Chinese-led MCP, the Chinese guerrillas and the Chinese victims; on the other, the Malay constables, the Malay troops of the government forces, the Malay officials and civil servants. Anthony Short describes the ethnic breaches of the conflict

> [The] outcome of the insurrection depended upon which side the Chinese would support: the campaign was itself a contest for their allegiance. At the same time, the defeat of the insurrection was due to the Malays: to their active support of government police, special constables, soldiers and so on: and to their passive resistance to what, for them, was usually regarded as an alien uprising.[7]

As the Emergency was fought to eliminate an enemy largely Chinese, it created a new peril for the rural Chinese, a peril with a strong ethnic flavour. Facing daily hardship, they could be forgiven for thinking that this was another chapter in the British–Malay alliance, another instance of government brutality – say, in the eviction of squatters – where Malay policemen and troops played a large part. The MCP had tried not to be drawn into such narrow racialism. Like all good communists, MCP leaders had no doubt made a spiritual investment in class universalism and cosmopolitanism. However, if the Chinese folk were to be protected from government abuses, the MCP would inexorably drawn into the ethnicist cauldron of 'Chinese against Malays'. There seemed no way out. If the MNLA guerrillas had to kill government troops, their victims would most certainly include Malays.

Over time, the MCP made itself a party of predominately Chinese leadership and rank and file members.

BUT LOOKING BACK AT its beginning, the MCP didn't look like this. The early Chinese communists had tried to build alliances with the Malays and Indians. In the last years of the 1920s, the NCP – Nanyang Communist Party, the MCP's predecessor – came into contact with Malay sections of the League Against Imperialism, a loose, multi-ethnic anti-British coalition. In 1929, a delegation of NCP organizers and Malay leaders – including a religious teacher from Malacca – travelled to Shanghai for the Pan-Pacific Trade Union Secretariat, held from July to August that year. There the delegates presented the problems facing the labour movement in Malaya, singling out the difficulties in bringing the various ethnic groups and their representatives into the unions. The

---

7   Anthony Short, 'Race and politics in Malaysia', *Asian Survey* 10(12), 1970, p. 1081.

Malayan delegates were arrested when they returned, prompting the CID, the Central Intelligence Department of the Singapore police, to boast that it had taken into custody 'Malay ringleaders of the communist movement'. The NCP were unable make much headway in recruiting Indian members, however.[8]

The other 'cross-ethnic' influence came from the Indonesian Communist Party (PKI) across the Straits. Right until President's Sukarno's *Konfrontasi* to subvert the formation of Malaysia, contacts were made between the Malayan communists and the PKI. Chin Peng, in the 1999 seminar at the Australian National University, was candid about MCP–PKI friendship. In the short period between the Japanese departure and Indonesia's independence in 1949, PKI leaders sought refuge in Singapore to escape Dutch colonial government persecution. (Dissidents of foreign powers could not be arrested under the Banishment Ordinance.) The MCP also helped with smuggling arms to fellow communists in Indonesia. After the Second World War, Chin Peng met up with the PKI leader Mas Alimin when the latter passed through Malaya. Before smuggling him safely back, in the months before Mas Alimin's departure Chin Peng put him in touch with the Malay nationalists, and got him to help set up a Malay Marxist training school. Chin Peng was sparse with the details, though you sense this was the extent of the MCP–PKI collaboration. 'A lot of Indonesian communists came over and stayed' Chin Peng lamented, 'but the problem was they did not stay permanently in Malaya. Had they done so, the MCP's Malay work would have developed much more.'[9]

The secretary-general was perhaps stretching the facts to make a point. For it had been a major myth of the MCP that, as a vanguard of the socialist movement, it had the serious intention to bridge the Chinese–Malay–Indian divide in the anti-colonial struggle. Something like the PKI–MCP link also helped to burnish the revolution's cross-ethnic reputation: 'Socialism for all Malayans!' In this the MCP would strike against the communal parochialism long nested in the colonial policy of 'divide and rule'.

During the Emergency the government, in the busy churning of its propaganda machine, was wont to reduce the conflict into one between two domestic

---

8   C.F. Yong, 'Origins and development of the Malayan Communist Movement, 1919–1939', *Modern Asian Studies* 25(4), 1991, pp. 644–5,

9   Karl Hack and C. C. Chin, *Dialogue with Chin Peng: New light on the Malayan Communist Party*. p. 72. For a history of the MCP–PKI relationship, see Cheah Boon Kheng, *From PKI to the Comintern, 1924–1941: The apprenticeship of the Malayan Communist Party: Selected Documents and discussion*. New York: Southeast Asia Program, Cornell University, 1992.

opponents: between communist terrorists (CTs) and defenders of democracy; between a godless, foreign-inspired ideology and a pious and loyal indigenous community. The government was careful not to mention the communities involved. Nonetheless, official propaganda helped to breed the understanding that CTs would be Chinese, while Malays would not join the MNLA guerrillas.

Speaking only of one side of this symmetry, for many Malayan people a Malay communist insurgent could be a strange, incongruous beast indeed. When the leading Malay communist Mohammad Indera, alias Mat Indera, was captured after his coffee was spiked with a hallucinogenic drug, it made the headlines. Mohammad Indera was a member of the MCP's Johore–Malacca Border Committee, and he had planned the 1950 assault on the Bukit Kepong police station near Muar, Johore state.[10] His capture sorely tested the official publicity machine, while the present Malaysian government have erased his person and ethnicity altogether from the official history of the Emergency. In the popular film *Bukit Kepong* (1981), the assault on the police station was carried out by Chinese terrorists, heroically resisted by the Malay constables and their families; the film makes no mention of Mohammad Indera.

The MCP, for its part, was attuned to the symbolic gestures that would broaden its cross-ethnic appeal. With acute perspicuity, the party would bring its few Malay leaders into the public eye whenever the opportunity presented itself. In December 1955, Chin Peng left the jungle and arrived in Baling town to attend a two-day negotiation with the Malayan and Singaporean governments to iron out a possible ceasefire and political settlement. At Baling, Malaya's number one (Chinese) CT presented himself, as did the Malay member of the MCP delegation, the cold-faced, taciturn Abdul Rashid Mydin, the one-time commander of the all-Malay 10th Regiment of the MNLA, who sat through the meeting in inscrutable silence. The MCP also had a Malay chairman, the CD Abdullah of our opening story. He would be a key signatory of the 1989 peace agreement between MCP and the Thai and Malaysian authorities. On another note, when the MCP's clandestine Radio Suara Revolusi Malaya, The Voice of the Malayan Revolution, first broadcast from Hunan Province, southern China, in 1968, it did so in three languages: Malay, Mandarin and English.

Compared with the Malays, the ethnic Indians seemed a richer ground for MCP agitation. Large numbers of ethnic Tamils worked in the rubber estates and in the railways; they were active in the labour movement before the Emergency. S.A. Ganapathy, a veteran of the anti-Japanese resistance, was the

---

10 Ibid., pp. 165–6.

first president of the 300,000-strong Pan Malayan Federation of Trade Unions (PMFTU), where CD Abdullah cut his political teeth. Ganapathy's career was cut short when he was hanged in 1949 for possession of arms. The other prominent ethnic Indian communist was R.G. Balan, who attended the Empire Conference of Communist Parties in London in 1947 with three other MCP representatives. Arrested and detained for ten years under the Emergency Regulations, he was elected in absentia vice-president of the MCP in 1955. He was released in June 1960, by then a broken man of thirty-nine, eager to renounce communism and reunite with his family and his aged mother. Another prominent ethnic Indian communist was P. Veerasenan, a committee member of the PMFTU and president the Singapore General Labour Union. He joined the MNLA when the Emergency was declared but was killed by the security forces in 1950. 'Veera' is Tamil for bravery, and to this day Tamil estate workers commemorate his life with the annual Veera soccer cup.[11]

However, neither the prominent Malay and Indian communists nor the near mythical Malay 10th Regiment of MNLA could change the essential Chinese character of the communist movement. The MCP was shrewd in presenting the insurrection it led as a broad cross-class, cross-communal struggle. However, Malaya's ethnic pluralism was a near insurmountable hurdle. For all the talk of the cross-ethnic comradely links, one feels that the MCP, as much as its sympathetic commentators, did not face up to the theoretical and tactical problems involved in ethnicity.

FOR MARXISM CLASS RELATIONS are the engine of radical social change. Capitalism pits those who own the means of production against those whose labour power contributes its profit. It is relationship fraught with contradictions, as the antagonism and potential violence brings a society to periodic crises and eventually to its total transformation. To class relations and their powerful social effects, the authors of *The Communist Manifesto* add an international dimension. In their ringing phrases, they proclaim the international nature of the proletariat movement:

> The working men have no country. . . . National differences and antagonisms between peoples are vanishing gradually from day to day, owing to the development of the bourgeoisie, to freedom of commerce, to the world market, to uniformity in the mode of production and in the conditions

---

11 www.malaysia.net/sangkancil/2000-09/frm00053.html. Accessed 16 April 2011.

of life corresponding thereto. The supremacy of the proletariat will cause them to vanish still faster. United action, of the leading civilised countries at least, is one of the first conditions for the emancipation of the proletariat.[12]

In *German Ideology*, Marx reiterates the same sentiment: '[W]hile the bourgeoisie of each nation still retained separate national interests, big industry created a class, which in all nations has the same interest and with which nationality is already dead.'[13] This sounds like a version of globalization, one with the transformative power of capitalist modernity thrown in. But in his view, the might of capitalism's production fashions a powerful force, whose logic and very freedom would erase the narrow framework of nation-states. In the same vein, the working class, as the vanguard of world communism, would elevate international class unity above 'patriotism'. 'Workers of the world, Unite!' and 'The working men have no country' are powerful voices of communist humanism: the idea that revolution should ultimately bring socialism to workers everywhere, not only to those in the home society. Thus, some Marxists are wont to regard nationalism as parochial and a thorn in the flesh of working class internationalism. The Polish-born Jewish intellectual Rosa Luxemburg, for example, was so exuberant about working class internationalism that she opposed Poland's independence from Russian rule. Internationalism also led her to dismiss the struggle for sectarian identities, including Jewish identity, which, to her mind distracted from the primary task of bringing down capitalism and the founding of socialism–communism.[14]

For Marxists like Luxemburg, nationalism and collective identities are clannish and partisan. Enemies of world working class solidarity, they thwart the progressive forces of international socialism. Yet, the facts bear out that even in an established communist state people still owe their allegiances to forms of solidarity other than class, playing havoc to the building of a socialist state based on class and national egalitarianism.

After the overthrow of the Tsarist State, the Bolsheviks found themselves facing the problem of how to deal with the national minorities whose cultural and religious attachments made a mockery of class unity. The question was: Should the revolution allow the 'self-determination' of these people, giving

---

12 Karl Marx and Frederick Engels, *The Communist Manifesto*, New York: International Publishers, 1948, p. 28.

13 Karl Marx, *The German Ideology*, Moscow: Progress Press, 1964, p. 76.

14 For a short, succinct rendering of Luxemburg's position, I find useful Christopher Hitchens' 'Red Rosa', *The Atlantic*, June 2011, pp. 1–9.

them a degree of cultural and political autonomy under the aegis of a central communist state? If so, would not this compromise the class solidarity central to the Marxist orthodoxy? Stalin's famous essay, *Marxism and the National Question*,[15] written in 1913 in Vienna under Lenin's tutelage, was an attempt to address the problem of 'nations within a nation'. Its aim was to lay out a political system which would bring the nationalities of Tsarist Russia under the single framework of a Soviet Union. Stalin was fittingly anthropological when he spoke of each nation as 'a historically constituted, stable community of people, formed on the basis of a common language, territory, economic life, and psychological make-up, manifested in a common culture'.[16] Stalin's recognition of national or ethnic differences was, we might say, an advance on Luxemburg's disdain for the parochial self-possessiveness of nationalism and sectarian identities. Stalin's central idea was not an argument for self-determination for Russia's minorities, however. As it was worked out later, the 'National Question' was resolved by way of the Federation of the Union of Soviet Socialist Republics (USSR). Under the constitution, each member 'nation' enjoyed nominal autonomy but near absolute state power was invested in Moscow. As the Soviets entrenched their power, national self-determination became a byword for reactionary ethnic self-fixation, and Stalin's brutal suppression of national minorities was one of the darkest chapters of the history of the Soviet Union.

THE MCP PRODUCED NO Marxist theoreticians that we know of. It is nice to imagine Chin Peng or CD Abdullah, as they rested in the jungle camp, safe from the pursuit of security forces, pondering over the problems of carrying out a Marxist revolution in a place like Malaya. Whatever their answers, we know the MCP had tried to mobilize the masses across the ethnic lines but did not altogether succeed. By the 1950s, nationalism was no longer the 'enemy' of world proletariat solidarity as was once thought. In the wave of postwar anti-colonial movements, the new generation of revolutionaries would see national self-determination as a part of the worldwide struggle for justice and political freedom. The days of the narrow take on the national question were gone. However, in each newly independent state the ghost of Luxemburg cast a shadow: tribalism. If national interests did not impede world revolutionary

---

15 Joseph Stalin, 'Marxism and the National Question', in *Works*, Moscow: Foreign Languages Publishing House, 1954, Vol. 2, pp. 300–81.

16 Ibid., p. 303.

movements, internally ethic attachments and parochialism were a harbinger of narrow sectarian divides, a foe of national integration. Tribalism was the new opiate of the people. The 'national question' had not really gone away.

As the MCP planned to build a 'socialist Malaya', we might wonder what its political choices might have been once it had taken power. Would a 'Socialist Malaya' go the way of 'the federation of nations' of the Soviet model? Should Johore or Perak take a 'nation status' because of their Chinese majority; and should Kedah and Terengganu become 'Malay states'? These were futile, impossible options. Among other things, unlike the Soviet Union, in Malaya ethnic communities did not live in their own territorial enclaves. 'A federation of Malayan socialist states', if it eventuated, would be spatially in disarray. In any case, the Soviet federation model would also mean the carrying over of the divisive 'each ethnic community for itself' of the colonial rule. Still, the MCP could indulge in bit of dialectic fantasy: once the revolutionary chaos had settled, ethnic differences and antagonism would organically melt way into the melting pot of socialist, class solidarity.

'History before the fact' is not irrelevant. As the MCP had vowed to bring about a 'socialist Malaya', the form it would take, and how it would affect the lives of Malayans, are legitimate concerns. The concerns show up the complex social and cultural factors facing every revolution. 'Oppressed Chinese labourers, Indian workers and Malay peasants, Unite!' – it would have been a bewitching cry for mass mobilization; but the MCP's failure to reach out to the Muslim Malays would have made a travesty of it. The best we can say is that while the MCP was undoubtedly for class universalism, conditions on the ground were against it. As they tried to extend a hand to the Malay left, they found a fractured political alliance, ideologically uncertain and anchored down by age-old communal preoccupations.

In his memoirs, CD Abdullah traces the shaping of his young mind that guided him to his revolutionary career. He writes:

> Several factors influenced my early political development. One was my knowledge of history, particularly of Malaya. The other was my close relationship with family and friends who were interested in the same issues. I was also lucky to get to know Indonesian revolutionaries who were seeking refuge in Malaya. These early influences fanned my decision to participate in the anti-British struggle . . .[17]

17 *Memoirs of CD Abdullah, Part one: The movement until 1948,* p. 8.

The Perak Rebellion had affected many Malay youths of his generation because it was a Malay struggle, a sacrifice of Malay lives and Malay blood. Like the legendary Perak warriors, they wanted, in CD Abdullah's words, 'to bleed in defence of [our] race and motherland'.[18] During the Japanese invasion, young Malays like CD Abdullah were radicalized by the British defeat in Malaya. Some joined the Union of Malay Youth (KMM), which for a time took part in the MCP-led anti-Japanese resistance. As was typical of other Malay nationalist associations, the KMM cast a keen eye on the aim of national independence. In what would have been for the Chinese a repugnant moral trade-off, the KMM eventually sought collaboration with the Japanese military authorities in return for their sponsorship of an 'independent Malaya'.

We know quite a lot of the KMM because of the career of CD Abdullah, and the writing of one of its founders, Mustapha Hussain (1910–87). His *Memoirs*[19] makes tortuous reading, half nostalgic rambling, half defence of KMM's scandalous role as fifth columnists for the Japanese. Also Perak born, Mustapha Hussain began his working life as an Agricultural Assistant before taking up a teaching post at the government School of Agriculture. In 1938 he and other young Malays from the elite Malay College Kuala Kangsar formed the KMM, with himself as the vice-president. As he recalls in his memoirs, 'KMM was founded by a group of radical left nationalists in their twenties. Influenced by world history in general and Turkey in particular, they desired a political body similar to the Young Turks.'[20] As for his anti-colonialism, he was moved by the poverty of the Malay masses, which he saw as the result of British neglect and the indifference of the Malay elite themselves.

> Even as children, we were exposed to heart-wrenching stories of early Malay struggles against British colonialists. The pathetic living conditions of Malays around my home stirred me to ask: 'Why do Malays have to live in deprivation while their motherland is literally overflowing with natural resources? As the Malay saying goes, "How come chickens in a rice store are starving, and ducks dying of thirst in the water?" What does the future hold for these gentle, refined and cultured Malays?'[21]

---

18 Ibid., p. 11.

19 *Malay Nationalism before UMNO: The memoirs of Mustapha Hussain*, Kuala Lumpur: Utusan Publications, 2004

20 Ibid., p. 18.

21 Ibid., p. 7.

Mustapha Hussain's fiery contentions were directed at British colonialism.

Receiving his particular ire was the colonial policy of admitting hundreds of thousands of immigrants into Malaya – the origin of the pathetic 'starving chickens in the rice store' situation of the Malays.

After the fall of Malaya in January 1942, Mustapha Hussain led a KMM delegation to Kuala Lumpur to ask the Japanese authorities to declare Malaya independent, citing Japan's promise to liberate Asiatics from European rule. The Japanese turned town the demand. They would prefer, under the Greater Asia Co-Prosperity Sphere, to extend their patronage to the people of Malaya, and not only the Malays. 'Let the Japanese be the father. Let the Malays, Chinese and Indians be the children,' one Japanese officer said at the meeting. 'However, if the Malay child is thin, we will give him more milk.'[22]

Not discouraged, later, in 1945, Mustapha Hussain worked secretly to draw up a Constitution of Independent Malaya that was to be discussed at a conference of Malay nationalists in August. As with Chandra Bose's Provisional Government of Free India, the Japanese military success presented the KMM with an opportunity to speed up independence. But events were moving fast. The tide of war was turning against the Axis powers and the Japanese surrendered on the fifteenth that month. The plan for an independent Malaya came to nothing; the KMM had played a dangerous game and lost.

After the war, the KMM leaders could not escape the reputation of having been Japanese collaborators. The president Ibrahim Yaacob prudently fled to Indonesia, but Mustapha Hussain was arrested and spent a short spell in prison. It left him a broken man. The Agricultural School sacked him from his job, and for a period he was banned from taking part in political activities. Jobless, he took to street hawking, and later worked as an insurance salesman. He entered the contest for power in UMNO, but was outmanoeuvred by players better connected and with less-stained reputations. He saw Malaya's independence arrived in August 1957; history had denied him a share of the glory. He died one night in 1987. Delirious with fever, as he wrestled with the ghosts of his past, flapping the arms like 'a turtle turned upside down', while his wife tried to hold him down ...[23]

The Mustapha Hussain/KMM story captures the convolutions of communal desires, Malay destiny, and – it always returns to this – the hurt and economic deprivation caused by other communities. For the Malay nationalists,

---

22 Ibid., p. xi.
23 Ibid., Introduction by Insun Sony Mustapha, p. xv.

since the British had been free and easy with admitting immigrants into the country, the struggle against colonialism would take on an anti-Chinese stance. Unavoidably, they would make the installation of Malay rights and privileges one of their key political agendas. Independence was nothing without the Malays gaining their special place in post-colonial Malaya.

Burdened by the notion of Malay sovereignty under threat, Malay nationalists had, as a remedy, looked afar and sought coalition with other Malays in the region. They were drawn to the rough-hewn idea of a 'federation of cultural Malays', the so-called *Melayu Raya* – Greater Malaya or *Indonesia Raya* – Greater Indonesia.[24] Since the early twentieth century, the idea of the 'oneness' of British Malaya and Dutch Indonesia had been current among Malay intellectuals. Many believed that the people in the wide arc stretching from the Moluccas across Borneo and Sumatra to the Malay Peninsula formed a single community, a single race. *Melayu Raya* had existed long before the arrival of European colonialism, they argued, which had broken off this unity of race and region. If Malaya and Indonesia were the homelands of a single race, the idea of a pan-Malayism could cement a federation of the two Malay-dominated nation-states. It was an exalted political fantasy, one which could be traced back to the racialism of British orientalists like Stamford Raffles. (The former Prime Minister Dr Mahathir Mohamad would add to the Malay World the people of the Philippines, the Malays in Sri Lanka as well as the Cape Malays in South Africa.) *Melayu Raya* or *Indonesia Raya* was an approach of 'safety in numbers' to strengthen the destiny of the Malays as a single people, just as it helped to battle what were perceived as the 'causes' of Malay deprivation.

The Malay left have remained a phantom in the history of anti-colonialism in Malaya, their significance or impact hard to pin down. From early colonial times until their demise in the late 1950s, they went through dazzling transformations, perked up by racialism and the perceptions of communal grievances. The KMM was beset by opportunism, internal dissension and unrealistic political goals. The Union of Malay Youth typified those Malay leftist parties that envisioned a regional Malay 'union' or 'federation' that would promote Malay interests. In this endeavour, freedom from colonial rule would be the first step, a political prerequisite in the struggle for Malay sovereignty. The KMM was not alone in this. So troubled were their voices, so overwrought their racialism, that Malay nationalists of all shades would put aside any assault on the

---

24 A good discussion of early Malay nationalism is Firdaus Abdullah, *Radical Malay Politics: Its origins and early development*, Kuala Lumpur: Pelanduk Publications, 1985.

Malay feudal order symbolized by the sultans. The struggle for Malay rights and cultural and religious identity was the greater aim. One is moved by how elegiac, how full of contradictions is the marriage of Malay nationalism and anti-colonialism. The final expression of this is probably offered by the Malay Nationalist Party or *Partai Kebangsaan Melayu Malaya*. A major anti-British, Malay organization founded in 1945, the MNP declared in its constitution the agendas: 'To unite the Malayan races, to instil the spirit of nationalism in the hearts of the Malays and to aim at uniting Malaya within the larger family i.e. the Republic of Indonesia.'[25]

Some of us in Malaysia are fond of harking back to a golden era of a pan-Malayan left during the decade 1945–55. After the declaration of the Emergency, the MCP, through its front organizations, continued to foment a struggle against the government, particularly in urbanized Singapore. Internationally, the early fifties saw a global wave of anti-colonial movements. In Asia the 1955 Asian–African Conference in Bandung, Indonesia, that brought together leaders like Nasser, the Egyptian strongman, Chinese Premier Zhou Enlai and Marshal Tito, president of Yugoslavia, signalled a new optimism for a non-aligned, socialist future in the region.[26] For the MCP the communist successes in China and French Indochina were a great boost of confidence. For a while, the Malay nationalists were caught up with the upsurge of anti-colonialism in the Arab world – Iraq, Syria, Algeria. The Chinese radical Lim Chin Siong openly declared support for the nationalist struggles in South Africa and Algeria. A cosmopolitan spirit and an internationalism seemed to have risen from the ashes of colonial 'divide and rule' and ethnic self-interest.

Lim seemed to symbolize the new spirit: he embraced comradeship with the Malay activists, writers and journalists, and he called for the Chinese to learn Malay, which he saw as a unifying national language for Malaya. As an informant tells it, young Chinese took to studying Malay as a 'revolutionary project'. She recalls a room filled with a conspiratorial air, with young men and women drilling themselves in Malay words and phrases, their faces glowing by the light of a kerosene lamp. When Lim died in 1996, those who came to mourn his passing were his friends and fellow political detainees: the sociolo-

---

25 Khoo Kay Kim, 'The Malay left 1945–1948: A preliminary discourse', *Sarjana*, 1(1), 1981, p. 187.

26 Sunil S. Amrith lays out the significance of the Bandung Conference among the Malayan left in 'Internationalism and political pluralism in Singapore, 1950–1963', in Michael D. Barr and Carl A. Trocki (eds), *Path Not Taken: Political pluralism in post-war Singapore*, Singapore: NUS Press, 2008, pp. 37–57.

gist Syed Husin Ali, the writer Usman Awang, the journalists Samad Ismail and Said Zahari, all ethnic Malays; the ethnic-Indian unionist A. Mahadeva and M.K. Rajakumar, a former leader of the Labour Party of Malaya (LPM); as well as his Chinese friends and colleagues.

Cosmopolitan and culturally sophisticated, Lim has long settled into the legend of the Malayan socialist struggle.[27] There had been no one quite like him. In Lim we invest a sort of martyrdom because he symbolized a socialist movement that almost succeeded. Lim and his personality press on our minds, for his cross-ethnic talent was rare among the Malayan left. Lim, we are tempted to say, had tried brilliantly to practise the class universalism of Marxism. His political base was urban Singapore with its large, diverse working class population. The MCP, deep in a Maoist guerrilla war in Malaya, had difficulty in transcending its ethnic-Chinese character. Socialist idealism and revolutionary rhetoric were present, certainly. But to build a truly multi-ethnic communist movement, to recruit greater Malay and Indian leaders and supporters called for a realistic assessment of the prevailing conditions. In the post-revolutionary state, communism hoped to sweep away the cobwebs of traditions and feudal attachments, but the people in that state always seemed to be dragging their feet. In post-Deng China, as evidenced by female infanticide in the villages, the 'national question' has not really lost its pertinence. Anthropologists have tried to pin down the causes – the primary determinants – of the pluralistic rift in a national state. But the enduring relevance and intensity of ethnic self-definition seems to defy the conventional explanations; colonial history, culture, and current political and economic forces have not really helped to find the answer. Ethnic cleavages are 'a phenomenon in its own right, a social force not reducible to other social forces'.[28]

We are wont to bemoan the MCP's failure to mobilize the masses across ethnic lines. But the hard question is, how could it have done this? It is a question we ask not only about Malaya. Class consciousness that leads to working class unity is an alluring idea of Marxism. In truth, people sharing the same experiences of oppression and exploitation do not necessarily unite and act as one. As Stalin realized in his morally perverse way, the oppressed Russian peasants were attached to their conservative ways. Feudal, communal values did not magi-

27 For a tribute to Lim, see Tan Jing Quee and Jomo K. S. (eds), *Comet in the Sky: Lim Chin Siong in History*, Kuala Lumpur: ISAN, 2001.

28 Adam Kuper, *Anthropology and Anthropologists: The British School in the twentieth century*, New York: Routledge, 1980, p. 240.

cally wither away under communism. Seen in this light, the parochialism that affected the Malayan left appears natural and perhaps inevitable, even though wider social and political forces did much to nurture it. We may also say that to overcome the forces of ethnic parochialism Malayan communism ought to have demanded of its leadership tough ideological wisdom. And ideological wisdom would have been needed in post-revolutionary Malaya. For as the Stalinist Soviet Union and Maoist China had shown, doing away with the feudal past is not a matter of a dialectic march to the future, but a bloody human affair. So perhaps the MCP's failure to build a cross-ethnic communist movement may not have been a bad thing since it brought about the movement's collapse. In the nether land of 'Socialist Malaya', if the MCP had taken power, what awaited Malayans, beneath the veneer of a socialist paradise of communal peace, might have been ethnic cleansing and something else murderously similar.

8 On Junglecraft
Britishness and the 'Flaming East'

The truth is that the jungle is neutral. It provides any amount of fresh water, and unlimited cover for friend as well as foe – an armed neutrality, if you like, but neutrality nevertheless. It is the attitude of mind that determines whether you go under or survive.
– Spencer Chapman, *The Jungle is Neutral* (1949)

[The] 'Flaming East' in all its gross materialism . . . shabby and intricate grandeur . . . and overmastering allure.
– Charles Allen, *Tales from the South China Sea* (1983)

In Malaysia and Singapore, we are accustomed to see the Malayan Emergency as a more or less straightforward narrative, starting with the MCP uprising in 1948, the British initial confusion, then the arrival of Templer whose leadership and energy turned the war around, before the government's final victory in 1960. Yet, like all human events, the Emergency cannot be captured by a neat register of events. War is a labyrinthine undertaking for all participants, one that often defies synthesis and generalization. I was reminded of this when I read *The Guns at Last Light: The War in Western Europe, 1944–1945*[1] by the Pulitzer Prize-winning historian Rick Atkinson. Concerning the Battle of the Bulge, Atkinson writes, : '[War] is never linear, but rather a chaotic, desultory enterprise of reversal and advance, blunder and élan, despair and elation. Valour, cowardice, courage – each had been displayed in this spectacle of a marching world.'[2] And he might have been commenting on the Malayan conflict when he states: '[V]ictor's justice, tinged with the sour smell of sanctimony, is a reminder that honor and dishonor often traveled in trace across a battlefield and even a liberator

---

1   New York: Henry Holt & Company, 2013.
2   Ibid., p. 491.

could come home stained if not befouled.'[3] *The Guns at Last Light* belongs to that genre of war history abounding in individual soldiers' experiences: their fear and suffering, their struggle for survival, their elation at victory. The book is about these as much as about the planning and execution by the general staff in launching a campaign. With journalistic verve, Atkinson takes the reader to the battlefield and the men fighting there, affirming: 'Even as armies and army groups collide, it is the fates of soldiers that draw the eye.'[4] A book like *The Guns at Last Light* taught me to give the Emergency a human face, by shifting attention to the individual solder or insurgent, by entering the consciousness, as it were, of combatants on both sides. The ethnographic encounter with the ex-insurgent Xiao Hong in an earlier chapter was written in this spirit. Moved by her self-revelation, I had in mind the need to amend her comrades' bland, self-serving tales as told to visitors at the Peace Villages in southern Thailand.

Ironically perhaps, the narratives of the British soldiers sometimes turn out to be more faithful to the facts. They do not go for the socialist realist mode; and I suppose, as victors they can afford not to grind the ideological axe. Shedding their anti-communism, Britishers could give over simply to recounting what they confronted daily. Take, for example, this description of a jungle trek by a British officer:

> Our introduction to *belukar* [the bush] was an education in itself. We found that only way through this heart-breaking stuff was to jump into it and hold it down while the rest of the patrol walked over you, each man repeating the process so that the patrol moved caterpillar fashion. On a good day we reached a speed of 100 yards per hour. We also learn to wade through swamps (chest high for sergeants: chin high for men) to avoid snakes, red ants, hornets and far more than fifty-seven varieties of non-timorous beasties; and to marvel at the ingenuity of leeches as they devoured our soft parts and occasionally dropped into our glass of ale back at the base.[5]

This is secondary jungle, regrown after logging and windthrow, that covers eighty per cent of the Malay Peninsula – a trackless wilderness of sunless gloom, and sheer misery. As if a reward for those who seek it, the primary jungle offers a different countenance, a different experience of the Malayan

---

3   Ibid., p. 13.

4   Ibid., p. 491.

5   Brian Steward, *Smashing Terrorism in the Malayan Emergency*, Kuala Lumpur: Pelanduk Publications, 2004, p. 198.

Colonel Freddie Spencer Chapman – naturalist, adventurer, 'Lawrence of Malaya'. (Source: unknown.)

wilderness. For nature lovers the primary jungle can be stunningly beautiful, with tree trunks hundreds of feet high, rising skywards like the columns of some great monument, its roof a wild green canopy. The Malayan jungle can offer great beauty, a wonder of the natural world. A Britisher with a certain metaphysical turn of mind could no more resist the Malayan jungle than T.E. Lawrence could escape the allure of the Arabian desert. During the Emergency the Malayan jungle was very much a place of ambushes and patrols that tested the endurance of the British servicemen. But for a person with the right sensibility, here one could also lose oneself in romantic reverie. This is a story of the Emergency not often told: how the attitude of British men and women defined their experiences of the Malayan wilderness, and in the process rewrote the idea of themselves and the Empire.

The book that immediately comes to mind here is Spencer Chapman's *The Jungle is Neutral*.[6] Part war memoir, part ethnographic observation, part 'boy's own adventure', the book recounts the two years the author spent with the MAJPA guerrillas during the Japanese occupation. Chapman never fought in

6   Spencer Chapman, *The Jungle is Neutral*, London: Chattto & Windus, 1950.

the Emergency, but he trained the Malayan Chinese guerrillas supplied and equipped by the British to form stay-behind parties after the Japanese victory. Another book of the 'British in Japanese-occupied Malaya' genre is *Pai Naa: the Story of Nona Baker* by Dorothy Thatcher and Robert Cross.[7] This is a quite different book from Chapman's. It is the story of an English woman, the sister of a tin miner, trapped together in the jungle by the Japanese invasion. Like Chapman, she and her brother found sanctuary in a communist guerrilla camp. Every line of *The Jungle is Neutral* is delivered in the prose of the British military memoir – formal, 'stiff upper-lip', and business-like. *Pai Naa,* on the other hand, weaves a tragic tale of sickness and misery as the two siblings struggle to survive in circumstances alien to them. Unlike Chapman, Nona Baker became close to her guerrilla-benefactors in way perhaps only a woman could. Chapman had his bird-watching while waiting for the Japanese troops to fall into an ambush; the highlight of the audacious British woman's guerrilla career was when she took up the baton for the MPAJA camp choir . . .

NONA BAKER ARRIVED IN Malaya in 1939 to join her brother Vincent ('Vin'), manager of the Pahang Consolidated Tin Mine at Sungei Lembing, north of Kuantan on the east coast. Vin was divorced, and Nona had come to look after him and keep house at the grand manager's residence. A parson's daughter accustomed to genteel frugality, she found at Sungei Lembing a sumptuous life of servants and gardeners and endless rounds of tennis and drinks at the club. *Pai Naa* portrays a young English woman, simple in her enjoyment, charming in her ease with the rhythm of colonial social life. She was an 'uncomplicated person'. While Vin was often gloomy over his failed marriage, and stressed over the welfare of his miners, Nona was all sunny temperament. She was practical and not given to brooding, and found no attraction in British colonial jingoism – unlike those in her social circle.

The Malayan Chinese communists came into the Bakers' lives when the Japanese invaded Malaya. At first they hid out in the jungle, living in a hut built by a couple of miners who also brought food and news from the outside. After a year, with increasing Japanese patrol, they decided to leave their hideout and seek sanctuary with the Chinese guerrillas they knew were operating in the area. Their helpers knew where their camp was; they were MPAJA sympathizers who had been bringing supplies and intelligence to the camp two hours' trek away.

---

7   Dorothy Thatcher and Robert Cross, *Pai Naa: the Story of Nona Baker,* London: Constable, 1959.

Nona Baker, the British 'girl guerrilla' of Malaya. (Source: unknown.)

On arrival, the Bakers were befriended by the commandant Lao Liu, a kind and light-hearted man – untypical for a communist, she is quick to note – and fond of eulogizing the workers' paradise in Stalin's Russia. He knew Vin, who recognized him as the union organizer who had once led a miners' strike in Sungei Lembing. Now, at the camp, they could laugh and joke about their reversed fortunes.

For their safety, Lao Liu moved the Bakers to a bigger camp about four hours' march away. Here, in the new place, they learned to adjust to the life of a guerrilla base. They were given special food – eggs, chicken and pork bought from the village – to supplement the camp diet of vegetables and tapioca. They joined Mandarin classes. They engaged in discussions with Lao Liu and corrected his many misconceptions about the conditions in 'capitalist England' – child labour was still being used, ten-year-old boys went down the mines, the poor had no vote and so on. Nona's metamorphosis began with her being measured for a new uniform. She was fitted for a shirt and a pair of khaki drill shorts, and for her feet a pair of shoes with soles cut out of smoked rubber sheets. The final touch was the khaki cap, with three red stars representing the major 'races', Malays, Chinese and Indians, that made up the MPAJA.

The Bakers were soon again on the move. Lao Liu feared losing them when the Japanese intensified their attack. The Sungei Riau camp was the largest they had lived in; it was the headquarters of the MPAJA regional command, with a parade ground and an office equipped with a typewriter, a duplicating machine and stocks of stencils, ink and paper, all rescued from the empty rubber estates and mines. Nona Baker found herself slowly drawn to the men and women in the camp, many of her age. She responded to their humour and kindliness and recognized their bravery in fighting a brutal enemy. She underwent no ideological conversion, however. She continued to be infuriated by the camp leaders' ranting about the virtues of communism and the achievements of the Soviet Union under Stalin, and by the easy way in which they dished out the death penalty. Once, when a stranger was found wandering near the camp, he was captured and summarily bayonetted to death. On another occasion,

MPAJA guerrillas wearing khaki caps with three red stars. (Source: photo still from film footage reproduced in the 1998 BBC documentary, 'Malaya - the Undeclared War', online at www.youtube.com/watch?v=pBRMRf0JVJc.)

after a lengthy torture, four old comrades who had stolen pork from the camp kitchen were tied to the trees and executed.

At this point, the narrative turns rhapsodic as it relates the homespun ordinariness of camp life – the cooking; the joy when a piece of meat went into the pot of stew that enlivened the diet of sweet potatoes, tapioca, rice and salted fish; the daily political lectures. And she tells about her hosts' almost child-like enthusiasm for dancing and singsong. At a request for a dance of the 'European style', the brother and sister would execute a waltz on the dusty parade ground while she hummed 'The Merry Widow Waltz', to great applause.

Later, seeing her talent in adapting herself to camp life, the commandant got her to start an English newsletter, to be distributed outside the camp. Nona had joined the guerrillas on various missions, but working on the newspaper was something special. It took her ever closer to the life of the camp, and it made her feel useful when time hung heavily over her and Vin. Under the direction of the 'rabid Communist' Ah San, her task was to start an English 'newspaper' for Malay and Indian readers, and for the Chinese who could not read the communist leaflets in Chinese. In the office Nona had the use of a typewriter, but ribbons were scarce. Sometimes she had ribbons and no carbon paper, and all copies had to be individually typed or hand written. The first issue came out in January 1945, in fifty copies. It was so popular that the commandant soon ordered an increase in production to seventy copies.

The news came from various sources. There were other camps with radios and transmission sets. Once, an American with a receiver set had been dropped by parachute and landed a few miles away, and patrols were sent to meet him in the other camp and get the latest news of the war. The other source of news was more ingeniously the local Japanese newspapers, except that the opposite of the claims of Japanese or Axis victories was printed. She went along happily with Ah San's editorial direction, reporting the epic struggle at the Eastern Front where the Soviet Union was single-handedly winning the war against Hitler.

With her song writing and camp chorus, writing and production of the newsletter, she kept herself busy. Earlier, she had had to force herself not to think of the past, and kept in check her runaway imagination as she pondered on her future if she fell into Japanese hands. She had little time for all that now. And she had created a bit of 'English culture' in the guerrilla camp with the ballroom dancing and singing – even though she had to change 'a moo-moo here and a moo-moo there' in 'Old MacDonald had a Farm' to the more up-lifting 'one-leg here and one-leg there' to commemorate a successful grenade attack on a Japanese staff car.

But what of her brother Vin? Much of *Pai Naa* is given to telling the gradual decline of the British planter, whose death in the jungle is full of pathos and a sense of the tragic. Vin was seventeen years older than his sister. After studying mining in Cornwall, he came to Malaya in 1911 to work for the Pahang Consolidated Company. He married an Australian woman and they had three children. But she was not happy in Sungei Lembing; she was listless and the climate did not suit her. Eventually they decided to live apart and she took the children with her back to Australia. A mining manager in British Malaya, all of six feet and with broad shoulders: Nona had looked up to Vin with sisterly pride. However, when she arrived in Sungei Lembing, she found him a somewhat lonely man, wifeless and doleful, living in a large gloomy house. As compensation, his energy was wrapped up in the mine which he ran with a firm paternalistic hand. To the workers, he was 'king and father'. He appeared reserved and somewhat forbidding, but he was also kind and scrupulously fair, qualities that earned him respect and a degree of loyalty from the miners. All the same, Vin was not the stiff-jawed, emotionless type. When he was in one his 'moods' he would chain-smoke and fill the house with his edginess; and he agonized over things. While Nona tended to go by instinct, 'Vin would not dream of deciding anything until he had looked at all sides of the question',[8] his sister notes.

When they first moved to the jungle, they thought they would hide out only for a few weeks, six months at the most, before the British retook Malaya. The fall of Singapore nailed the coffin of this optimism. The ever loyal Cheng Kam, Vin's foreman, with two kindly old men, Wong Ng and Lau Siu, built them a hut and over the following months came for visits and brought supplies and news. Vin had been their boss, but now he and his sister were dependent on them. Still, their life was not intolerable. They had enough food and the trio's visits kept up their spirits. Later, when they moved deeper in the jungle to avoid Japanese patrols, Vin remained cheerful about the future. He talked about the plan he had for the mine when he returned: how he would drain it, restart the pump, and salvage the bags of tin he had dumped at the bottom of the mine. He would work hard to restore his beloved community. In the wet, dim hut on a rainy day, it was Nona who missed the Sungei Lembing home, the social life, the club.

It's hard to say exactly when Vin began to slowly lose his mind. Perhaps it was when Cheng Kam brought news that Singapore had fallen. Vin was

8 Ibid., p. 7.

stunned; 'he walked a little way into the jungle and stood leaning against the tree in an attitude of utter despair', Nona recounts.[9] The return to the mine was now a fantasy, and the prospect of being captured or killed, or years of living in the jungle, had become very real. And what would happen to them if any of their helpers were arrested and revealed their whereabouts? Or perhaps he began to lose it when they were forced to move from one primitive hut to another. The desperate flight and dissipated hope made Vin morose and depressed. For days he would not speak, and no amount of Nona's coaxing could bring him out of his mood.

Their settling in the communist camp had solved the problem of survival. Food was plenty, if bland and uninspiring: sweet potatoes, tapioca, vegetables, though rice was rigorously rationed, and meat of a monkey or an elephant when rifle shots could be risked. Security was improved, and there was, of course, human company other than themselves. There were things to do. Nona, through her own personality and skill, made herself useful. At the camp, she underwent a striking transformation as she took to the 'communist work ethic' of the guerrilla base.

For Vin life was different. He was a man who had once played 'monarch' to his men in Sungei Lembing, who both loved and feared him. He was used to giving orders and quick to dismiss as 'humbug' anything that interfered with his work. At the camp, all the flag raising, morning assembly and concerts were communist cant; unlike his gregarious sister, he could not make himself join in. As a European man he was rarely asked to do very much, certainly not 'undignified' chores like cleaning and cooking and peeling sweet potatoes. Perhaps his air of a white colonialist, or simply his clumsiness at menial jobs, freed him from being busy. Occasionally, they would use him to make maps showing the paths and tracks in the area he knew well, but these tasks were short and few and far in between.

His guerrilla hosts were sticklers with their rules of hospitality, but lack of work left Vin idle and restless. Without work he was not a part of the camp. Removed from the mine and his workers, he had already lost his former world and the social status that went with it. In the jungle base, his situation made the point: without work he was near nothing, and the carpet of existential certainty had been yanked out from under his feet.

The middle months of 1943 saw a series of Japanese assaults on MPAJA bases all over the peninsula. The communist leaders decided to break up the

---

9 Ibid., p. 39.

Sungei Riau camp and move deeper into the jungle. Vin, already sick with beri-beri and dysentery, was in a feeble state and an insect bite had swollen one of Nona's legs, making it painful for her to walk. They could not follow the guerrillas to where they were going. So a hut was built for them in the thick of the jungle and a messenger was to bring food and supplies from time to time.

Friendless and alone, their stay in the jungle was hell. The hut was poorly erected, without sleeping platforms, and torrential rain would make a river of the muddy floor. When the messenger fell ill or failed to turn up, they went without food, sometimes for days. Life became an endless series of miseries. The abscess on Nona's leg had broken, and from her knee to ankle was one long suppurating sore. Dysentery was getting worse for both; too weak to walk outside the hut, Vin would lie at night in his own excrement.

The end came one early morning. She used the last match stick to start a fire for warmth and to heat some water. She held him to her skinny arms and cried. But Vin was insensible to Nona's effort to comfort him; in his unconscious state he twitched his legs violently in the death throes. The Chinese messenger had just arrived; he watched Vin's slow, fitful breathing and shook his head. 'I sat bolt upright and let out a piercing yell,' Nona Baker tells of her brother's death, 'which echoed round and round the jungle wall and set up a raucous chatter from the monkeys.' His body went limp, and she hauled herself away to the other side of hut. As she waited for the burial party to arrive, she started to eat: '[I]t is a measure of my stunned, weakened state of mind that I was able to sit by the dead body of the person I loved best in the world, and eat slowly and deliberately the piece of pork which the Chinese had brought that morning.'[10]

THE STORY OF THE Bakers claims a place in the Emergency narrative if only for Nona's candid portrait of the Malayan communists still some years away from being anti-British insurgents. The communist camp was not all the time preoccupied with indoctrination and uplifting songs and speeches, even though there were plenty of these. In Nona's account, the MPAJA men and women come across as a gregarious and fun-loving lot. They played ball games and held concerts and told jokes. They tortured and executed spies and stealers of food, but they were also kind to the villagers and paid for what they took. And the MPAJA were, to all appearances, skilled guerrilla fighters. They were always ready to move, never letting the temporary comfort of a camp tie them down. They kept to a network of jungle paths and *attap* huts safe from enemy

---

10 Ibid., p. 142.

patrols. With fickle radio sets, they stayed in touch with other MPAJA units and kept themselves informed of the progress of the war. Time and again, it was the guerrilla's nose for danger and quick manoeuvre that saved the Bakers from being captured by the Japanese. The survival of 'Malaya's only English girl guerrilla', as the press was to dub her after the war, was due as much to Nona Baker's own sturdy-mindedness as to her protectors being assiduously drilled in security and quick manoeuvres.

We owe a good deal to Nona Baker for her affecting tales about life in a communist camp in pre-Emergency Malaya. Yet, in the end, it is Vin's lonely death that is to me most evocative. Allowing him a degree of literary grandeur, Vin symbolizes something of British colonialism itself. Rubber and tin are like the silver mine in Conrad's *Nostromo* that bewitches and brings the Europeans to their doom.[11] Vin, when I think of him, calls up those Conradian figures – Kurtz, 'Lord Jim', Nostromo – burdened with the bad faith of being a white man in an alien world. His descent into dejection and death seems to have come out the pen that has given us some of the most powerful portraits of imperial greed and human frailty in pursuit of the Great Enterprise.

In Conrad's *Heart of Darkness*,[12] on the voyage to join the steamboat he has been commissioned to captain, the narrator Marlow is sickened by the behaviour of his fellow passengers – their avarice, their treatment of the Africans, their self-justifying colonial attitude, their idleness on board. Later, on his own riverboat, facing the dark forest along the River Congo, he feels a sense of man's inner corruptibility signalled by the jungly gloom threatening to lure him in. What saves him is his duty on the boat. As captain, he cannot 'abandon ship' – Conrad's great metaphor of bad faith – to indulge in a bit of howling and grovelling before the fetish ashore. The solidity of work anchors him down; it keeps at bay the imagination always lurching towards excessive, unbridled thoughts.[13]

In *Pai Naa*, work also featured prominently in the lives of the MPAJA guerrillas. The socialist principle of 'food for those who labour' was enforced. Those who failed to do their assigned chores did not eat, though the sick were fed and cared for. Most people in the camp worked to be useful, not only to

---

11 Joseph Conrad, *Nostromo*, New York: Dover, 2002.

12 Joseph Conrad, *Heart of Darkness*, London: Penguin, 1995.

13 There is another side of this, though. The safety of the boat also prevents Marlow from experiencing the depth of human evil that only moral debauchery can reveal, as shown by the brilliant and messianic Kurtz. Marlow is saved by his work and, for that, falls short of the tragic grandeur Conrad invests in Kurtz.

gain food. And being useful gave each person a place in the social order and kept everyone safely on board the 'Conradian ship'. In communism's puritan creed, labour builds and produces and also, like the furnace in a steel mill, purifies and casts out the dregs. If this sounds remarkably similar to Vin Baker's attitude, it is because the Victorian imperial ideology that provided the seed of his values also upheld the redemptive power of work and industriousness. For, as historian Martin Lynn has shown, between 1830 and 1850, as the Empire shifted to free trade it began to turn to actions and policies that took 'military, naval, religious and *cultural* forms'.[14] The bride of free trade is the idea of 'capitalism as a moral force'.[15] The affinity of free trade to capitalism propelled the confidence that the imperial undertaking would 'innovate' and 'civilize' the world, while instilling a work ethic among economically – and morally – backward people globally. It is this imperial ideology which had moulded Vin's mind and values.

Perhaps it is fitting that Vin Baker should meet his end in the jungle. He was beset with disease and depression. But he was also in a place where he could not meaningfully work, and without work he was a 'non-person', a person shorn of significance. Vin in a jungle camp is a different figure from those that fill the Emergency narrative, full of purpose and soldierly resolve. Yet, the Malayan conflict at the end of Empire signalled the demise of the heroic imperial figure. Anthony Burgess's Malayan trilogy *The Long Day Wanes*[16] published from 1956 to 1959 is set in the last days of the British in Malaya. The author is so full of sneer for his characters – both British and Malayan – that their moral feebleness comes across as common and unremarkable. After *The Malayan Trilogy*, in the sixties we had *The Virgin Soldiers* by Leslie Thomas. The book, a bestselling comic potboiler, tells its story from the point of view of the young national servicemen for whom British imperial pretensions held no cachet. Like his fellow national servicemen, Private Bragg spends much his time bellyaching about the hardship of the jungle. After a sweaty patrol in a fruitless search for insurgents, only ice-cold Tiger Beer and the embrace of Juicy Lucy or one of her sisters-in-trade can undo the sting and exhaustion. The collapse

---

14 Martin Lynn, 'British policy, trade and informal Empire in the mid-nineteenth century', in Andrew Porter (ed.), *The Oxford History of the British Empire: Volume III: The Nineteenth Century*, New York: Oxford University Press, 1999, p. 103. My emphasis.

15 Ibid.

16 The three books are: *Time for a Tiger* (1956); *The Enemy in the Blanket* (1958); and *Beds in the East* (1959). Reissued: London: Vintage, 2000.

of the Britisher in the tropics, and with that the fall of the Empire's moral posturing, is complete.

STILL, THE BRITISH IMPERIAL figure could also be brave, stoic and audacious. An empire builder, he transformed the Victorian beliefs into personal values. He was a man who thrived on hardship, whose inner qualities were tested by the African wild, the Arabian desert or the Asian jungle. In these places, the imperial ethics found an expression not in work as such but the arduous undertaking he had set out to accomplish. In Malaya, one such story of the lion-hearted imperialist tells again of involvement with MPAJA guerrillas, but he was of a different mettle from Vin Baker and Private Bragg.

Spencer Chapman's profile facing the title page of *The Jungle is Neutral* shows an elegant head; the cheek lean and slightly sunken, the eye alert and looking forward as though the mind is thinking about some task ahead once the sitting with the artist is over.

Colonel Spencer Chapman DSO ('Freddie') was one of the British military types who could wear many hats on his head – adventurer, expert in guerrilla warfare, scholar. He is sometimes compared with T.E. Lawrence of 'Lawrence of Arabia' fame, both soldier-philosophers given to solitude, emotional detachment and ambiguous sexuality. Before the war, Chapman made his name in a series of expeditions to Greenland, the Arctic and the Himalayas; he was also private secretary to Basil Gould, the Political Officer for Sikkim, Bhutan and Tibet. He spent six months in Tibet, an experience that produced two books, *Lhasa: The Holy City*[17] and *Helvellyn to Himalaya*.[18]

In August 1941 he arrived in Singapore to command the No. 101 Special Training School to prepare men for guerrilla operations in the Far East. When the Japanese launched the attack on Malaya four months later, Chapman proposed to the authorities a plan to set up stay-behind parties using MCP volunteers. His superiors were not keen – to them the talk of stay-behind parties sounded defeatist and the plan involved arming the communists. As the Japanese marched rapidly down the peninsula, the authorities changed their mind. Chapman moved the school across the causeway to Kuala Lumpur where he began training some twenty young communists who, supplied with arms and explosives, formed the first detachment of the MPAJA. Thus began the strange relationship between the British and the MCP that was to last until after the war.

---

17 London: Chatto & Windus, 1938.

18 London: Chatto & Windus, 1940.

The Jungle is Neutral is sparse with details about the MPAJA men and women. Unlike Nona Baker, Chapman is too stiff-jawed to give us the human side, the child-like idiosyncrasies of life in a communist camp. But he notes that the communists were disciplined and trustworthy, if a bit humourless. And he never doubted that their protection had ensured the survival of him and his team. Instead the book turns largely to himself and the experience of deprivation he had endured. By mid-December 1941, Japanese troops were a third of the way down Perak, in north-west Malaya. Chapman's first thought was to 'have a look at the enemies' who were reputedly first-rate jungle fighters. With two companions he crossed the Perak River and spent four days watching Japanese troops on bicycles peddling south and towards the final target: the fortress of Singapore. 'This reconnaissance more than ever convinced me of the vulnerability of the advancing Japanese forces to guerrilla attacks,' he writes.[19] Chapman had his party building up stores at the jungle fringes at Tanjong Malim, near Kuala Lumpur, while he remained in the capital to organize provisions for other hideouts. On January 6 the following year, he experienced the first bout of illness that would plague him in the coming three-and-a-half years. After two days of high temperature and delirium, he felt sufficiently recovered to travel and cross the Main Range to join his party in Tanjong Malim.

The Jungle is Neutral describes the eleven-day march over fifteen miles – slightly more than a mile a day – to reach the camp. It was, as they say, an epic journey. The jungle terrain hindered the march at every slogging step. Chapman and his two British companions encountered no Japanese patrol; the enemy was the jungle which taxed their strength and navigational skill. He gave an account of the ordeal at a Royal Geographical Society meeting after the war.

> The going was worse than I had believed possible. We were continually climbing mountain-sides so deep that we had to haul ourselves up by roots and saplings and lower ourselves down the other side with rattan lines, and the only "level" places were valleys full of enormous boulders covered with treacherous layers of creepers and moss. Direction finding was surely more difficult than anywhere else in the world. . . . Moreover, in the dense jungle which limited visibility to about 50 yards there was no object on which to mark, so that we had to watch the compass continually; and even if a landslide or fallen tree provided a loophole through which we could obtain a view, we merely saw one blue tree-covered hill behind another fading into

19 Chapman, *The Jungle is Neutral*, p. 27.

the distance, and there was no way of identifying any one of these monotonous features with the myriad mountains shown on the map.

And the weather made misery of everything:

> It rained . . . almost continually and one of the worst results of this was that our matches, in spite of elaborate precautions, soon disintegrated so that we could no longer cook our meals, dry our clothes, keep ourselves warm at night, or, worse of all, keep at bay the voracious insects of the jungle. I had always imagined it was warm in the tropical jungle, but at night, though we made leaf shelters and wore all our clothes, we shook with cold beneath our sodden groundsheets, and in the morning our faces would be so swollen with the bites of mosquitoes and sand-flies that we had to bathe them in cold water before we could even open our eyes. Worse of all were the leeches; every night we had to remove some dozens of these revolting bloated creatures from the most tender parts of our bodies, and apart from the irritation of the bites, the loss of blood was considerable.[20]

When they reached the camp, the original party had vanished. Chapman tells what had happened to its members, one Chinese and three Europeans. The Chinese radio operator had gone his own way and the three European planters had escaped by boat to Sumatra, then to Singapore, still in British hands. In Singapore, he recounts, 'Hembry was ill but the other two, hearing that I had still intended to reach Tanjong Malim, returned just before the fall of Singapore to look for me.' 'Unfortunately', he tells the reader, 'they were caught by the Japanese. A year later they managed to escape, but on being captured were beheaded.'[21] What happened to them – illness, capture and death – more or less sums up the fate of Europeans living in the jungle as they waited for the British to return.

Over the 'Mad Fortnight' in February 1942, Chapman and his communist comrades attacked Japanese vehicle convoys, destroyed railway lines and bridges, and generally created an impression of a large guerrilla force in operation. Chapman was at his best. The craft he practised was what he had taught at the guerrilla training school. He and his team moved silently at night, laying delayed charges on rails and cutting telegraph wires. Once, after a successful ambush, he and another British officer each changed into a white shirt and a sarong around

---

20 Spencer Chapman, 'Travels in Japanese-occupied Malaya', *The Geographical Journal* 110(1–3), 1947, p. 19.

21 Ibid., footnote 1, p. 20.

the waist and disguised as Tamil labourers; passing by a Japanese patrol, they had 'whined to them in abject Tamil' – a Scarlet Pimpernel duo of the Malayan jungle.[22]

The next three-and-a-half years were less glorious. Like his fellow British officers, Chapman was ill much of the time. Once, on the run from the Japanese, he went down with malaria for two weeks in an abandoned aborigine hut. He describes one of the bouts of sickness that struck him and his companion:

[For] more than two months we were both seriously sick, running an extremely high temperature and being shaken by violent rigours. Fortunately our crises occurred at different times, so that we were able to look after each other to a certain extent. Luckily there were some M. & B. tablets in my medical set, and it was probably due to them that I did not die of pneumonia. There was also a thermometer, which gave such disquieting readings that at the time we thought it must be out of action ... In the morning during the attacks of fever which followed the rigours my temperature went to as much as 105 or even 105.5 degrees, so that in one day there might be a range of 10 degrees! ... On May 5th I felt so ill that I thought I was going to die, so I started to write my will but soon had to dictate it to Haywood – not that it made much sense.[23]

He collapsed soon after and lay comatose until May 23, seventeen days later. When he had recovered, he weighed seven or eight stones to his normal twelve. He examined his emaciated frame:

I would not have believed it possible to lose so much flesh and yet remain alive. My limbs were like chicken's legs – straight sticks with exaggerated bulges at the joints – my ribs and shoulder bones stood out, and my face was quite unrecognizable: deep hollows had appeared on my temples, and my cheeks and jawbones protruded like a skeleton.[24]

And adding to the misery, he was moving from camp to camp. In each new camp he found other Europeans – members of other stay-behind parties, odd British soldiers, a few American airmen shot down during a raid. They were all seriously sick: malaria, dysentery, beri-beri. Many were dying. Besides their illnesses, Chapman was struck by their poor spirits, their lack of will to go on,

---

22 Chapman, *The Jungle is Neutral*, p. 98.

23 Ibid., p. 140.

24 Ibid., p. 142.

as though ready for death's call. Chapman's verdict – for he is no Conrad – is curtly matter-of-fact and shorn of philosophy. With the Europeans, he was sure, it was their mental attitude that was slowly draining the life from them. He was harsh in his assessment of the chances of survival of the average British soldier in the 'green hell': a NCO perhaps a year, a private a few months or even a few weeks. Chapman sums up his view:

> There is one school of thought ... who see the jungle full of innumerable visible and invisible horrors – scorpions, snakes, and centipedes, deadly fevers, ferocious wild animals, and hostile natives. Then there is another, who think that the jungle is teeming with game, fish, and edible roots and fungi, and that branches of bananas and pineapples drop into one's lap. Both these viewpoints are equally false; but the jungle does provide unlimited fresh water and cover where Englishmen as well as Japs may hide. It is the attitude of mind that is all important: the jungle itself is neutral ...[25]

The Malayan jungle is no Eden, but neither does it absolutely condemn one to illness and death. For a person not in fear of the jungle, Chapman opines, it provides all one needs – fresh water, fruits, edible plants, shelter and effective cover from enemies. But it is the mental attitude – always for Chapman the key to his junglecraft – that calms one's terror of the jungle and allows one to turn to it for its rich offerings. For his eulogizing of the flora and fauna, he never gave over to romanticizing the Malayan wilderness. The jungle is simply, plainly *is*, neither hostile nor friendly. 'The jungle is neutral.'

IN HIS FOREWORD TO the book, Field Marshal Wavell praises Chapman for exemplifying the special kind of British soldier who excels in 'irregular and independent enterprises'.[26] 'Our submarines, commandos and air-borne forces ...', he writes, 'have proved that where daring, initiative, and ingenuity are required in unusual conditions unrivalled commanders and men can be found both from professional and unprofessional fighting men of the British race.'[27] Wavell has a point. The Second World War produced a spate of Special Operations groups led by men who prized independent action and self-initiative. The Long Range Desert Group (LRDG); the Special Air Service (SAS); the No.1 Demolition Squadron nicknamed Popski's Private Army after its founder, Major Vladimir

---

25 Chapman, 'Travels in Japanese-occupied Malaya', p. 36.
26 Field Marshal Earl Wavell, Introduction, in Chapman, *The Jungle is Neutral*, p. vi.
27 Ibid.

Peniakoff; the Chindits under General Orde that operated, in 1943 and early 1944, against the Japanese in Burma – they made their reputation with 'bold dashes' inside enemy territory, harassing the German or Japanese forces and disrupting their supply lines. However, like Churchill's Special Operation Executive (SOE) which was to 'set the flame ablaze across Nazi-occupied Europe', the human costs of these special forces were high when set against their achievements. The Chindits were especially controversial. In Operation Longcloth, Wingate's 1943 long-range penetration into Japanese-occupied Burma, out of the 3,000 men who took part, 818 – about a third – were killed, captured or died of disease.[28] Wingate would be one of Wavell's 'unrivalled commanders', and Churchill thought him 'a genius' and 'a figure quite above the ordinary level'.[29] But Wingate was also tempestuous and erratic, which might have contributed to the high casualties of his unorthodox guerrilla tactics.

When we think of British officers like Orde Wingate, Spencer Chapman and T.E. Lawrence, we search for words that would describe them. Words like 'mad' and 'messianic' come to mind; they seem to fit the qualities of Wavell's British warriors, albeit in a more intense, fervid sense. Chapman was, to a degree, 'mad' and 'messianic'. The signs were all there – the stoicism, the near-demented devotion to duty and the extraordinary zeal in carrying it out, the talent for solitude and imagination, the endurance of hardship as an art. Chapman alive in the jungle is light-years away from the wretchedness of Vin Baker dying in a pool of his faeces. Yet *The Jungle Is Neutral* is so devoid of self-doubt, its author so revelled in his punishing undertaking, that it gives us pause for thought.

Chapman's kind of Britishness was born of the English public school that strove, and still does, to produce future generations of the ruling class – 'patriotic, clean-limbed and high-minded'.[30] Administrators and servants of Empire, so it is often said, were made on the cricket field, and by a regime of cold showers and morning sermons. The English public school, which is really a private school, saw as its duty to produce men of integrity and serious ideals just as its teachings fostered an idea of 'the gentlemen, and the obligations of class'.[31]

---

28 Martin Brayley, *The British Army 1939–45: The Far East*. London: Osprey Publishing, 2002, p. 19.

29 Trevor Royle, *Orde Wingate: A Man of Genius 1903–1944*, London: Frontline Books, 2010, p. 203.

30 John Bayley, *The Power of Delight – A Lifetime in Literature*, New York: W.W. Norton & Company, 2005, p. 166.

31 Ibid;, p. 167.

What senses of responsibility and emotional affliction were instilled in these young men, the future runners of Empire! In the lonely outposts of Africa or Asia, discipline and emotional restraint were the qualities needed to carry out the daily administrative tasks, some exacting, others mostly humdrum. But the demand was not only in the colonial servants' self-belief, but also in their relationship with the natives. For each man on the spot not only had to hold on to the imperial ideals, he must appear so to the public world, especially the colonized people. The cultural side of colonial rule was all about public performance, about ritual and ceremony, in the way of 'making an impression' on the natives. George Orwell wrote in his classic 'Shooting an Elephant',

> [The white man in the colony] . . . becomes a sort of hollow, posing dummy, the conventionalized figure of a sahib. For it is the condition of his rule that he shall spend his life in trying to impress the 'natives,' and so in every crisis he has got to do what the 'natives' expect of him. He wears a mask, and his face grows to fit it.[32]

And when the mask becomes fused with the face reality and fantasy become one. The real self is hidden behind the mask, but the inner self can also be a 'posing dummy'. The 'hollow man' may well be the colonial servant marooned in an imperial outpost. One suspects that, for him, such is the nature of imperial power that to impress the natives is also to impress oneself. Again, Orwell,

> But even then I was not thinking particularly of my own skin, only of the watchful yellow faces behind. . . . A white man mustn't be frightened in front of 'natives'; and so, in general, he isn't frightened. The sole thought in my mind was that if anything went wrong those two thousand Burmans would see me pursued, caught, trampled on and reduced to a grinning corpse like that Indian up the hill. And if that happened it was quite probable that some of them would laugh. That would never do.[33]

For the young Orwell, to be laughed at by the natives would be a fate worse than death. The killing of an elephant running rampant is to him fraught with meaning, as he turns his gaze on to himself.

Unlike Orwell, Chapman is not the type of Englishman who would give over to the scrutiny of his deeper nature. But his telling of the Herculean trek

---

32 George Orwell, 'Shooting an Elephant', *The Collected Essays, Journalism and Letters of George Orwell*, vol. 1, Harmondsworth, England: Penguin, 1968, p. 239.

33 Ibid., p. 241.

across the Malayan jungle seems to have something of overcompensation about it. It is British understatement – a gentleman never boasts – with just a whiff of false modesty. Both men carried inside themselves an eggshell vulnerability, though only Orwell would admit it. Occasionally in British military memoirs, a successful venture warrants the accolade of 'a brilliant bit of soldiering'. Modesty is public school training. Making little of one's achievements is part of good manners, which invites praise. A strong character and correct will help one to survive in the wild, for to fail would be a failure to oneself, to one's class, to the Empire.

In the end, Chapman was nothing without the Malayan jungle. It is as if the 'extreme conditions' he experienced were so existentially affirming that when removed from them he chose death, socially and bodily. After the war, Spencer was headmaster in schools in Germany and South Africa, before taking up the wardenship of a hall of residence at Reading University, England. In his later life, he suffered bad health and frequent bouts of depression. Not wanting to be a burden to his wife and family, he shot himself in the head in his office, aged sixty-four.

9 On Writing People's History
Home-grown revolution

Who decides when (and if) the influence of imperialism ended?
– Edward Said, 'Always on top' (2003)

When I think of him, many years after he was killed, my mind brings up a young man, staid and austere, a brown gunnysack slung over his shoulder, which makes him stoop a little as he comes through the door. His countless visits to our house in Kuala Lumpur stay in my memory. When he came alone, he would drop the gunnysack on the floor and, after muttering some words of greeting, go off by himself. We never knew where he went and who his friends were. 'A strange boy,' my father would say, shaking his head, 'always running off somewhere.' But other times, when he arrived with his mother, there would be no shying away from the adults. He had to stay to suffer the ritual. Over the gracious jostling between our parents – 'Oh, you shouldn't have.' 'It's nothing. It's only a few worthless things from the farm.' – he would cut the manila rope at the top of the sack and let out the home-grown gifts. Potatoes, carrots, cabbages, onions, celery – things indeed of little value but convenient and affordable presents from the farm. They were our poor relations, and we were happy that they had not betrayed their sensible ways by spending money on American apples or Dutch biscuits, customary gifts of 'face'. The vegetables had travelled on a day-long bus journey and grit and dirt adhered to them still. For us, the gifts were honest and touching; they reminded us that Second Aunt had brought something of her life, something of her family carving out a living from the muddy hills of the Cameron Highlands. Living in the city we were pleased to have kin who were farmers, even though we were not privy to all that went on in their lives. It is easy for me, many years on, to think of the gunnysack as holding the sign of an existence that had somehow embroiled my aunt and her family in its peril and mystery.

We children called her Second Aunt and her son cousin, but they were not our blood-related folk. For it was the habit of Hakka people, small in number and in fear of rough handling by other Chinese 'tribes', to claim kinship with other Hakkas whose forefathers had come from the same village in China. The practice created 'fictive kin' out of strangers, an instant cementing of social bonds previously non-existent. My father was a keen practitioner of this an-thropological ploy. Over time, as the web of 'relatives' swelled, he never forgot the moral obligations that went with it. When news came that some 'sister' – it was women who more often needed his intervention – had fallen into difficul-ties in her marital home, where she was mistreated by her husband or mother-in-law, he would appear at the house and launch his rescue mission. His style was a subtle mixture of diplomacy and firm words. 'She is my Second Uncle's niece, you know. You can't treat her like that. You have to give me some face.' My father was for many years the chairman of the Hakka Association in Kuala Lumpur and a person of some influence. Often his intervention was enough to have the miscreant mend his or her ways. Other times, however, when the bit-terness had dug deep and the wife wanted nothing less than a separation, then an arrangement would be made for her to leave and find a home elsewhere. In this manner, my father made himself the rescuer of lost Hakka women.

At age fourteen, Second Aunt went to work as a maid in the house of one of our 'kinsmen' who had a lorry repair business in downtown Kuala Lumpur. Her mother had brought her up after her father died, and Second Aunt was made an orphan when her mother too passed away after a long illness. My father had arranged for her to board with the lorry repair family he knew. Later, it was suggested that there had been 'an understanding', according to which she was to be married to the family's youngest son when she reached eighteen. My father denied this. In any case, true or not, her adopted family had stuck to the out-dated notion of social chattel: having been fed and cared for, she was already 'owned' by her benefactor, and marrying into the family was a way of repayment, an expression of gratitude. As the son got older, encouraged by what the family regarded as a fait accompli, he began to turn his gawking attention towards her. It was a pinch here, a touch there, a cornering of her in the kitchen for a quick embrace. 'The young man's crude and uneducated', my father would say after one of his visits to the troubled home. 'He has breathed all his life the dank, greasy air of the lorry workshop; and she is such a lovely girl!' Once he had decided Second Aunt needed rescuing, there was no shirk-ing from what he had to do.

There were many tearful conferences between my father, Second Aunt and her adopted family in the following months. When it was decided that she would leave and live elsewhere, he found for her this time a 'salt of the earth' farming family in the Cameron Highlands, the hill station north of Kuala Lumpur, who would give her work and board. Though it was not a part of the plan, she later fell in love with their first son and married him. A year later a son came into the world, oblivious to the rough and tumble his mother had gone through. News came that he was healthy and growing up fast. One day during the Chinese New Year, the baby was brought to show us. The mother was creamy with happiness: fate had finally blessed her with a baby and a loving husband and turned her life around. I know all this from family stories – about my father's enterprise of mercy, about his selfless meddling in other people's lives, and about how Second Aunt and her son became a part of our life.

When the boy reached young adulthood, it was natural that my father would find a job for him in our Chinese herbal shop. He had gone to a high school in the Cameron Highlands, but he was not a good student. He skipped classes and picked fights with others in the schoolyard; and he was 'restless', Second Aunt's catch-all word for her young son's various misdemeanours. So at sixteen he was sent down to our shop to learn a trade and make something of himself.

Ours was a small business, and it adhered to the tradition of treating the workers like members of a family. Workers were fed three meals a day at a large table in the kitchen; dinner was served at five so that those with families could leave early. As for the young apprentices the shop was home: they took their meals there and, at night, slept on fold-up canvas beds wherever space could be found, dreaming their dreams next to the cartons of cod liver oil and Brand's Essence of Chicken and bales of poppy husks.

I was then about eight or nine, still in primary school. To my young mind, Second Cousin had just enough of silent mystery to make me hero-worship him. He was distant with my father; his face turned to a feint haughtiness when the older man spoke with him, as if to say, 'I live and eat here, but I work hard for you. There is no need for me to cringe and grovel at your feet.' Why he took to his boss's young son was a riddle. Perhaps it was my innocence, perhaps it was my incessant questions about many things that puzzled me. I wanted to know what lay beyond the clouds, and why a bicycle in motion did not fall. We spent a good deal of time together. We went to the movies; he helped me grow my stamp collection; and he took me to picnics in the park. In the company of his friends – young shop apprentices, students, clerks, a few teachers – he was free and boisterous like the rest, as if he had been released from the toil and stifling subservience demanded of him by our family shop.

Then events happened that had the effect of aiding his departure. First, he had an accident riding his bicycle with me on the crossbar; I had to have stitches on my elbow and spent half-a-day in hospital. He was unharmed and no one blamed him, not even my parents. After that, things seemed to slide. The oven caught fire when he forgot to douse the burning charcoal after he had finished roasting the herbs. A couple of months later, on the way to the bank with a canvas bag of two days' taking from the till, he was waylaid by a couple of thugs barely fifteen minutes away from the shop. One stuck a knife at his belly, the other freed the bag from his hand before taking off in a waiting car. It happened so fast, he later told the police, that he had not thought of resisting and could not remember their faces. At the police station, the detective told my father that he suspected Second Cousin was in it with the robbers. It had been too well timed, too perfectly executed without insider help, he said. The idea of a perfect heist went over my father's head, however. He could not believe Second Cousin was involved, nor would he sack the young man as the detective had suggested.

Second Cousin chose to leave of his own accord. He went back to his parents and the family farm in the hills. We heard news of him from time to time. From the farm he had gone to a tea plantation where he stayed for a year or so, then drifted back to Kuala Lumpur. He never got in touch with us. Once I saw him at a car park on my way to school, guarding and wet-wiping a Mercedes Benz. He looked at me and turned away, not recognizing me. The busy life caught up with us, and we began to think of him as one of the many young men who entered our shop and drifted away, who made a life for themselves by working in the city or setting up shops in small towns and villages.

Yet, I could not put him out of my young mind. I missed our conversations about the mysteries of the world for which he seemed to have all the answers. It had seemed to me even then that he should break out of my father's miserable shop; that his departure would be no betrayal of kin loyalty but the first step in a journey to something grander, though I had no idea what it could be.

The final piece of the jigsaw of his life was revealed to us one afternoon. Second Aunt had made one of her visits – the same long dusty ride on a bus, the same mud-coated gifts in a gunnysack, the same creamy happiness now bestowed on another son. In the sitting room, Second Aunt and my mother were crying, the tear-soaked handkerchiefs in their hands like flags of mutual sympathy. They interrupted their weeping and gave us the news of Second Cousin's death. He had joined the communists, my mother told me; he had been killed a few weeks before in a night ambush outside the family house when he made one of his visits. I can recall still the dark gloom of the late afternoon, the women's tearful sadness, as the normal conversation about their families gave over to mourning the demise of a young man dear to us.

Our safe, petty bourgeois existence had produced a revolutionary; Second Aunt, the suffering woman redeemed, had harboured an insurgent, her son.

Through Second Cousin, our family had become entangled with a world for us as foreign and distant as a star in the far-flung galaxy.

WRITING ABOUT THE EMERGENCY can be a bit like what Flaubert said about prose: it is a bitch; it is never finished.[1] It is hard to draw a line between the war and the everyday life of Malayans. We lived in the city, and the fighting took place in the countryside. What we learned of the 'communist terrorists' came from the newspapers and pictures of the slain they carried: each a limp, crumpled body contorted in grotesque form, bullet wounds visible on the blood-stained shirt. For us the fighting was somewhere else, someone else's business and folly. Yet, just when we thought the Emergency would not touch us, we were jolted into remembering our father's brief incarceration, and Second Cousin's killing. Our sense of security was unhinged.

Second Cousin remains for me an enigma. The best I can come up with is the power of imagination which, for some, channel personal discontent into political action. Was the dusty work he shared with his fellow apprentices his primary 'working class experience' that willy-nilly propelled him towards a revolutionary path? He was our 'home-grown revolutionary'; and he had brought us face-to-face with the Emergency in its murderous reality. At Adelaide University, he seemed to have presided over my choice of courses, as if I had opted for the study of Marxism and political economy in his memory. And there is a certain truth when I say that he had hovered over my shoulder as I did my anthropology fieldwork among the poor fishermen on Cheung Chau Island, Hong Kong, and that he had fortified my flagging spirits as I lay miserable and seasick below deck of a fishing junk on a voyage to the Gulf of Tonkin. If I exaggerate, I blame it on my hero-worship of him, which seems to affect me still.

In my early academic career, I, like so many, was drawn to the New Left of the Frankfurt School and French Marxists like Althusser. Their call for a cultural and psychological understanding of power and class relations, we thought, had the power to change the world by a new form of radical politics. It was the Sixties and I was a different person from the young boy at the shop on High Street. 'Armchair Marxism' had launched me into a compelling terrain, just like Second Cousin's transformation from a meek shop apprentice to a communist

---

1   The actual line is: 'What a bitch of a thing prose is! It's never finished; there is always something to redo.' Gustav Flaubert, *Madame Bovary*, London: Penguin, 2010, Introduction, p. vii.

insurgent. To the discomfort of my older colleagues, I was sure the 'cultural turn' in Marxism was no less worthy than the enterprise of those who braved the bullets and got their boots dirty in the jungle. Years on, the ideological climate has changed, and so has my extravagant faith in revolution. And the thought sometimes comes to me: my martyred Second Cousin was lucky not to have lived through the Cold War; what would he have made of Stalin's murderous regime and the fall of the Berlin Wall? Second Cousin was a man who had, with his comrades, taken part in a battle against the might of the British Empire. In my romantic yearning, I envy him for staking his life on a grand undertaking that has no parallel in our age of postmodern, global capitalism.

However, in thinking about revolution and about someone like Second Cousin, a little scepticism is not a bad thing. History has made us evaluate more realistically communism and its doings. Is that why my encounters with the ex-MCP guerrillas at the Peace Village seemed to carry a sense of catastrophe? We talked, and they smiled and answered my questions before falling back on the party line. I wanted to seize the conversation and get them to talk about something more revealing about their lives and the revolution itself. I wanted to know how they felt about sacrificing the prime of their life in the jungle fighting the British. When I asked the question, the answer came back pre-packaged, and just a little bit too smoothly: 'We have not wasted our youth. We fought against the British and without us Malaya wouldn't have got independence so early.' On the other hand, though, I would have been even less forgiving had they, all weary and mournful, recanted their violent past. No one is endeared to a turncoat. In my mind, I wanted them to keep their ideological faith, yet discern communism's moral and political failures. They should, I thought, take stock of the costs of communism and bring it to account.

During one of my visits to southern Thailand, I stood with an old comrade before the Martyrs' Memorial that commemorates the 1970 purging of alleged spies and counter-revolutionaries thought to have infiltrated the MCP (some 200 MNLA men and women were executed and more stripped of their ranks).[2] It was past midday, the boiling sun was beating down on our heads. I was an academic on a research trip, he a retired insurgent living out his twilight years. We were both historically out of place and irrelevant. We were both pathetic figures before the great height of the Memorial, with the red stars and inscription looking down at us. The MCP's homicidal errors were imbedded in each dent of the grey ugliness.

---

2   Karl Hack and C. C. Chin, *Dialogue with Chin Peng: New light on the Malayan Communist Party*, p. 24.

For a moment, I asked myself: Are the historians right? Were these people killed to ape the struggle at the height of the Cultural Revolution in China?

In the end, we do not take the Peace Villages' aged residents to task, because they are the only revolutionaries we've got. I think of the young students hovering over the communist 'uncles and aunties' in the restaurants, their ears tuned to the stormy tales of revolutionary ardour coming freely, fervently, from the mouths of the elderly. The tales maybe a tad self-serving, but they feed the need of the listeners seeking out a different history of the communist insurrection. If the official narrative is singularly pro-British and pro-government, then the 'people's history of the Emergency' is more expansively an expression of several things: the search for national identity, the need to understand the origin and meaning of Malaya's only revolution, socialist nostalgia and 'red tourism'. The alternative history of the Emergency can be the Malayan version of the *Olstalgie* ('nostalgia for the East') that is found in the former East Germany and other parts of communist-Eastern Europe. The Malayan communist revolution failed. The MCP's struggle for political recognition in the early postwar days, its capitalizing on the party's reputation as heroes of the anti-Japanese resistance, the MNLA fighters' bloody sacrifices in the jungle – they came to nothing. Yet, there lies the romance. At any Peace Village, before a complicit audience, the tales of fanatical hope and epic endurance festooned the magnificence of the MNLA guerrillas. In such a retelling, a 'Socialist Republic of Malaya' doesn't seem such a far-fetched and inconceivable idea after all.

Communists were fundamentalists even before the term 'fundamentalism' came to popular use. With all that has been written about and experienced in the communist state, its absolutism and ideological orthodoxy come across as the tread of a savage beast. The wheels of the state were propelled by an unshaken belief that nothing should impede the march to the Socialist Paradise; no social and moral costs were too high to assist its final arrival. There is no getting away from the fact of the communist faith in the dialectic of history. For Marx and his disciples, communism was to take the form a political *project*; it demanded a 'master plan', a time-line, an ideological commitment from its followers for whom sacrifice and blood were the highest expression of their calling. Even before the fall of the Berlin Wall, given the near genocidal measures of Stalin and Mao against their own peoples, it was hard to look at Malayan communism – any communism – with a naïve, innocent eye. At the ANU dialogue, no one thought of asking the secretary-general: what plan did the MCP have for Malaya once it had expelled the British? Would the MCP have gone the way of labour camps and 'struggle sessions' in cleansing the reactionary elements of the old regime – all those Malay policemen and civil servants, the pro-British Chinese elite of the MCA, those informers and collaborators sieved from the miners and estate workers. Historians have the adage 'the past in context', but that should not mean avoiding the reassessment of an event readily fallen into myth. Historical hindsight is a great clarifier not because everything of the past is an open book, but because the present forces us to look back and re-examine those events that still fill us with disquiet and wonder.

SOME YEARS AGO, IN Singapore, the then Senior Minister Lee Kuan Yew invited some of us from university to attend his lecture to a foreign delegation. The awaiting recipients of Lee's expansive wisdom were a group of trade unionists from post-apartheid South Africa. The badly suited men – ex-ANC guerrillas, I was told – and a few women had come to experience the magic of the Singapore economic miracle. Perhaps the island republic's bluff confidence could be transported back to South Africa to inform its own economic planning. Settled in a velvet-covered chair of the Equatorial Hotel, the glacial breath of air-conditioning biting into my neck, I steeled myself for the irony. In the front seats below the podium were victors of the struggle against white South Africa, men and women who had survived a bush war; and they had come to take counsel from the leader of a nation of some four million people (it was around 1998) to whom nationhood had been handed on a platter by the departing British. (I once asked a sour-looking man of the Vietnamese delegation during one such briefing: What could they, people who had beaten the French at the Battle of Dien Bien Phu, possibly learn from Singapore about how to run a shoe factory?) It was a mutually complicit game, however. The black South Africans were humbled by their new, non-soldierly tasks; and Singapore could garner some satisfaction by sharing its economic lessons with the former ANC guerrillas. What sealed the deal was Lee's speech. He recounted his own battle with the communists and leftists who had threatened to hijack Singapore's independence from liberals like him. Solemnly, Lee urged the new South Africa to adopt a West-friendly economic policy and invite foreign investment. Forget about the revolution, it should be business as usual as far as South African's capitalist economy is concerned, he counselled. That night, I took some ANC delegates shopping in Little India. We walked along the street under the gaudy neon lights; no one had anything to say about the lecture. I took their silence to be a sign of the distractions of the designer watches and portable sound systems, or perhaps it was an edgy discomfort for having to listen to a capitalism-friendly lecture they weren't quite prepared for.

Singapore and Malaysia belong to those postcolonial states which had not had to pay in blood for their nationhood. Blood and lives had indeed been spent, but in denying the communists the laurel of victory, not in a struggle against the Empire. The truth is that in both countries, the bourgeois leadership had inherited the nation on the cheap. Anti-colonial violence was not their way, and we know that Britain was ready to leave even before the end of the Emergency. Malaya was to be decolonized but not abandoned. The result was the transfer of power to a West-leaning regime fostered by defence pacts and special trade relations. The arrangement freed Britain from the responsibilities of Empire, and ensured that the major economic assets would remain in British ownership. National leaderships in Malaya and Singapore had their anti-colonial rhetoric, of course. But their enemy was communism, not the Empire. In the Emergency the interests of the nationalist leadership and the vestige of Empire were united.

The unities and oppositions between the Empire and its subjects make for a beguiling hall of mirrors. We in Malaysia and Singapore are the descendants of the early inheritors of colonial power, and some of us speak modishly of the dark stain of Empire etched on our collective soul. But many of us hold on to the feeling that British rule in Malaya, when we chance to think about it, was not so bad, really. Some among the educated, having read their Conrad and Fanon, know about European imperialism's moral debaucheries. But they happened elsewhere – in the Belgian Congo, in French Algeria, rather than *here*. We still believe, by and large, in the good story of the British Empire: its culture, its benevolence, its political generosity.

To my father, the best thing about the Empire is that it allowed people like him to accrue modest wealth by their own sweat and labour. The British rule he knew is like the great ocean on a calm day, indomitable, a bulwark against the threatening elements, while the children play safely on the beach. He had tried to live his own life, but the Empire had a way of complicating things. A loyal colonial subject, he had spent a day in jail on suspicion of aiding the communists, and his young 'nephew' had joined the revolution and died for the cause. People seemed to get caught up with the Empire, one way or the other. 'On both sides of the imperial divide men and women shared experiences – though differently inflected experiences – through education, civic life, memory, war', Edward Said writes.[3] This is as true for Malaya as for any European colonies. And speaking of 'shared experiences', had not the British

---

3   Edward W. Said, 'Always on top', *London Review of Books* 25(6), 2003, p. 3.

and their postwar enemies, the communists, once joined in fellowship in the fight against the Japanese?

In one sense, it was simply the nature of everyday life in Malaya. The British ruled and imposed their authority, while the colonized – and not only people like my father – lodged themselves in the system that oppressed as much as it protected life and property. The relationship was skewed, of course. Nonetheless a space existed between colonial administration and popular self-interest that conjoined the ruler and the ruled. In Malaya, the genius of British rule was that it left sufficient slack in the reins of control and oppression such that its benign intentions came through for most people. Call it mystification or what you will; that is how many thought, and still do, of the Empire. Malaya was rich in rubber and tin, and the harshness of exploitation and occupation was moderated by British liberalism, and by the pragmatic reason that tyrannical measures would not be efficient in making the most of the colony.

This is not backtracking to put in a few good words about the Empire. In an 'anti-imperialist' book such as this, one struggles with the question of how much the British were morally culpable for what happened in the desperate years of the Emergency. I have found the intellectual task daunting. Malaysia has produced the 'The West made me do it' grandiloquence made famous by the former Prime Minister Dr Mohamed Mahathir. But not every speck of the local interest – the Malay sultans, the ethnic community elites, the Malay–Chinese–Indian coalition that took power, the bourgeois beneficiaries of the colonial economy, the people that made their living from the tin and rubber industries – can be enlisted to spice up an anti-imperialist critique. In Malaya as elsewhere the colonizer and the colonized did share what Edward Said calls 'overlapping territories' and 'intertwined histories';[4] and these remain difficult to disentangle and reveal their social effects.

There has been, in recent years, a busy trading of 'soft-core Raj revivalism'. The chugging of the conveyor belt, as Said has pointed out, has delivered the BBC documentaries of Niall Ferguson and Jeremy Paxman, the Merchant and Ivory films, the fashion accessories.[5] The Malaysian contribution to the industry may well be the casual clothing brand East India Company, specializing in 'colonial era-inspired fashion'. East India Company's success led to another brand of Raj nostalgia: British India. The slogan that launched the company reads: 'Presenting British India. An era of racism, oppression, injustice and

---

4   Edward W. Said, *Culture and Imperialism*, London: Vintage, 1994, p. 72.
5   Said, 'Always on top', p. 3.

nice outfits'.[6] Its boutiques carry drill-khaki Bombay Bloomers, and men's suits and women's skirts and blouses in white linen, with antique topee sun helmets and saddles and polo sticks at the window display to lend each shop imperial glamour. I once bought a British India suit to brighten the drab days in the office, but an unease clung to my bodily frame. Still, this is only 'lifestyle consumption', like one's iPhone. Yet I dare say a kernel of meaning lies at the heart of it. To use the Empire to sell fashion feels like poetic justice, a postcolonial settling of scores. But it could also be a bland ignorance of the signs and significations of Empire and, with that, a brushing off of the need to bring it to account.

In these early years of the twenty-first century much has been happening in the former British colony. Prime Minister Datuk Seri Najib Razak has repealed the Internal Security Act created during the Emergency to detain without trial those deemed to threaten state security. The lifting of the law heralds a new era for the government after winning the April 2009 election. When the news was announced, the secretary-general of the opposition DAP (Democratic Action Party) Lim Guan Eng, an ex-ISA detainee himself, had called it 'epochal', but warned that the government 'should not try to dress up the old laws in new security laws'. The words proved prophetic. Since then new security laws have been put in place which still allow the executive the power of detention in terrorism cases. The Police Act, another Emergency measure, has been amended to permit freedom of assembly, but not street protests.[7] The old is lodged in the new, and the new has grown out of the old. As financial corruption accusations against senior government leaders, including Najib himself, grow apace, one finds it hard to argue that all these are the bequests of Empire. In form but less in substance, Malaysia has inherited from Great Britain a Westminster system of government, a legal system based on the common law principles, and a set of liberal cultural values and attitudes. If nothing else, we can say that the Empire has gifted to us a political and judicial apparatus to run a democratic state. Over the years, the formal features of government have changed. Many of the repressive laws had their origins in the Emergency Ordinances. But it is an exercise in pure cynicism the way these laws have been kept in the books, ready to be used against the

---

6   'British India founder wants to make it "a great company"', *The Star*, 21 December 2013.

7   www.themalaysianinsider.com/malaysia/article/najib-announces-repeal-of-isa-three-emergency-declarations. Accessed 24 August 2015.

opposition and dissidents when needed. The opposition leader Anwar Ibrahim's sodomy charge is based on the archaic 'law against the order of nature' of the East India Company; the sad affair says as much about the heritage of Empire as about the post-colonial state's perpetuation of it. A mixture of complicity, power and state self-interest, as well as history, explains the residuals of Empire still affecting our lives today.

As for the communist insurrection, it has become a roost of many things: ideological illusion, social myth, and state triumphalism. For the vanquished, the feeling of abjection is like a self-inflected wound, painful but worthwhile. There's nothing like an aborted revolution to coddle romantic nostalgia for those who had fought for the 'good cause' and lost. It seems to me remarkable that the conflict has invited so much mystification in way we think about the communist insurgents. For some they have taken on the mantle of national heroes, whose revolutionary violence hastened the granting of independence. Yet the writing of an alternative narrative of the Emergency, it is clear to me, should not concern itself only with redeeming the MNLA men and women and their reputation. More expansively, we should also appraise the political ambitions and tactical failures of the communist movement itself. We have to reckon with the fact that history has few kind words to say about communism in general. What happened in Stalin's Soviet Union and the catastrophes of Mao's China and Pol Pot's Kampuchea have dug the grave of Malayan communism in our assessment. But then historical hindsight may clarify too much. It too easily compares the state communisms and highlights their paralleled achievements and failures. All the same, the questions haunt us on the left: How can we project with certainty that 'Socialist Malaya' would not have gone the way of murderous socialist regimes elsewhere? Can we imagine, after the dust of the anti-British struggle had settled, the arrival of a 'people's republic of Malaya' free of ideological terror and homicidal violence? Perhaps a victorious communist revolution in Malaya would have turned out to be not much to celebrate.

Perhaps it is our modern sensibility. Nostalgia holds sway, and the mind turns away from what it sees as a flawed, corrupted present in order to seek solace in some lost illusionary Eden in the future. In this Eden, life will be secure, ideas and values spiritual rewarding, the leaders wise. We look towards to the future as a firm piece of ground on which to rest our feet after a hard slog through the mud of moral confusion. And communism had been the most eloquent expression of modernity. With the end of communism, the sociologist Zygmunt Bauman believes, the world is left without an alternative to capitalism.[8] But the reality is we cannot live without an alternative, and there are sufficient sins and moral viciousness in liberal democratic states that call for the leftist critique. In Malaysia and elsewhere, this may well be the significance of the communist past: for all its moral foundering, when shorn of its ideological orthodoxy, communism could offer the political lesson, the way of mass mobilization, in the fomenting of an anti-capitalist, radical dissent.

---

8   'Living without an alternative', *The Political Quarterly*, 62 (1), 1991, pp. 35–44.

Bibliography

CD Abdullah. 2009. *Memoirs of CD Abdullah, Part one: The movement until 1948*. Petaling Jaya, Malaysia: SIRD, 2009.

Abdullah, Firdaus. 1985. *Radical Malay Politics: Its origins and early development*. Kuala Lumpur: Pelanduk Publications.

Amrith, Sunil S. 2008. Internationalism and political pluralism in Singapore, 1950–1963. In Michael D. Barr and Carl A. Trocki (eds), *Path Not Taken: Political pluralism in post-war Singapore*. Singapore: NUS Press.

Atkinson, Rick. 2013. *The Guns at Last Light: The War in Western Europe, 1944–1945*. New York: Henry Holt & Company.

Barber, Noel. 1971. *The War of The Running Dogs*. London: Fontana.

Bauman, Zygmunt. 1991. 'Living without an alternative.' *The Political Quarterly* 62 (1): 35–44.

Bayley, John. 2005. *The Power of Delight – A Lifetime in Literature*. New York: W.W. Norton & Company.

Bayly, Christopher and Tim Harper. 2007. *Forgotten Wars: Freedom and Revolution in Southeast Asia*. Cambridge, Mass.: Harvard University Press.

Bennett, Huw. 2009. '"A very salutary effect": The counter-terror strategy in the early Malayan Emergency, June 1948 to December 1949.' *Journal of Strategic Studies* 32 (3): 415–44.

Brayley, Martin. 2002. *The British Army 1939–45: The Far East*. London: Osprey Publishing.

Burgess, Anthony. 2000. *The Long Day Wanes*. London: Vintage.

Callwell, Major-General Charles E. 1898. *Small Wars – Their Principles and Practice*. London: HMSO.

Camus, Albert. 1971. *The Rebel*. London: Penguin Books.

Carbaugh, Robert J. 2008. *International Economics*. Mason, OH: South Western Cengage Learning.

Chapman, Spencer. 1947. 'Travels in Japanese-occupied Malaya.' *The Geographical Journal* 110 (1–3): 17–36.

————. 1950. *The Jungle is Neutral*. London: Chatto & Windus.

Cheah Boon Kheng. *From PKI to the Comintern, 1924–1941: The apprenticeship of the Malayan Communist Party: Selected Documents and discussion*. Ithaca, NY: Southeast Asia Program, Cornell University, 1992.

Cheah See Kian. 2009. *Malayan Chinese Left Wing Literature: Its influence by China [sic] Revolutionary Literature (1926–1976)*. Penang, Malaysia: Han Chiang College. (In Chinese).

Cloake, John. 1985. *Tiger of Malaya: The life of Field Marshall Sir Gerald Templer*. London: Harrap.

Clutterbuck, Richard. 1966. *The Long Long War: The Emergency in Malaya, 1948–1960* London: Cassell.

Cohen, Michael A. 2010. 'The Myth of a Kinder, Gentler War.' *World Policy Journal* 27 (1): 75–86.

Conrad, Joseph. *Nostromo*. New York: Dover (2002 edn).

————. *Heart of Darkness*. London: Penguin (1995 edn).

Cross, John. 1957. *Red Jungle*. London: The Quality Book Club.

Curtis, Mark. 2003. *Web of Deceit: Britain's Real Foreign Policy*. London: Vintage.

Darwin, John. 1988. *Britain and Decolonisation: the Retreat from Empire in the Post-war World*. London: Macmillan.

Deery, Phillip. 2007. 'Malaya, 1948: Britain's Asian Cold War?' *Journal of Cold War Studies* 9 (1): 29–54.

Dobby, E.H.G. 1952. 'Resettlement transforms Malaya: A case-study of relocating the population of an Asian plural society.' *Economic Development and Cultural Change* 1 (3): 164–89.

Farwell, Byron. 1972. *Queen Victoria's Little Wars*. New York: Harper & Row.

Ferguson, Niall. 2003. *Empire: How Britain made the modern world*. London: Penguin.

Fisher, Charles A. 1964. *South-East Asia: A social, economic and political geography*. London: Methuen.

Flaubert, Gustav. *Madame Bovary*. London: Penguin (2010 edn).

Furnivall, J.S. 1948. *Colonial Policy and Practice: a Comparative Study of Burma and Netherlands India*. Cambridge: Cambridge University Press.

Gaiskell, Hugh. 1952. 'The Sterling area.' *International Affairs* 28 (2): 170–76.

Gallagher, John and Anil Seal. 1982. *The Decline, Revival and Fall of the British Empire*. Cambridge: Cambridge University Press.

Goffman, Erving. 1961. *Asylums: Essays on the social situation of mental patients and other inmates*. New York: Anchor Books.

Gregorian, Raffi. 1994. '"Jungle Bashing" in Malaya: Towards a formal Tactical Doctrine.' *Small Wars and Insurgencies* 5 (3): 338–59.

Gwynn, Major-General Charles William. 1934. *Imperial Policing*. London: Macmillan.

Hack, Karl. 2008. 'British intelligence and counter-insurgency in the era of decolonization. The example of Malaya.' *Intelligence and National Security* 14 (2): 124–55.

———. 2009. 'The Malayan Emergency as counter-insurgency paradigm.' *Journal of Strategic Studies* 32 (3): 384–414.

———. 2012. 'Everyone lived in fear: Malaya and the British way of counter-insurgency.' *Small Wars & Insurgencies* 23 (4–5): 671–99.

Hack, Karl and CC Chin, (eds). 2005. *Dialogue with Chin Peng: New light on the Malayan Communist Party*. Singapore: Singapore University Press.

Hamzah-Sendut. 1966. 'Planning resettlement villages in Malaya.' *Journal of Environmental Planning and Management* 1 (1–2): 58–70.

Han Suyin. 1960. 'Social change in Asia.' *Suloh Nantah: Journal of the English Society Nanyang University Singapore* 15–16.

Harper, T. N. 1999. *The End of Empire and the Making of Malaya*. Cambridge: Cambridge University Press.

Hastings, Max. 2004. *Armageddon: The Battle for Germany 1944–45*. London: Macmillan.

Hobsbawm, E. J. 1999. *Uncommon people: resistance, rebellion and jazz*. London: Abacus Press.

Horne, Alistair. 2006. *A Savage War of Peace: Algeria 1954–1962*. New York: New York Review of Books.

Hussain, Mustapha. 2004. *Malay Nationalism before UMNO: The memoirs of Mustapha Hussain*. Kuala Lumpur: Utusan Publications.

Hitchens, Christopher. 2011. 'Red Rosa.' *The Atlantic* June 2011: 1–9.

Jackson, Robert. 1991. *The Malayan Emergency: The Commonwealth's War, 1948–1966*. New York: Routledge.

Kenley, D. L. 2003. *New Culture in a New World: The May Fourth Movement and the Chinese Diaspora in Singapore, 1919–1932*. New York: Routledge.

Khan, Shamus Rahman. 2011. *Privilege: The Making of an Adolescent Elite at St. Paul's School*. Princeton: Princeton University Press.

Khoo, Agnes. 2004. *Life as the River Flows: Women the Malayan anti-colonial struggle*. Petaling Jaya, Malaysia: SIRD.

Khoo Kay Kim. 1981. The Malay left 1945–1948: A preliminary discourse *Sarjana* 1 (1): 162–192.

Khoo Salma Nasution and Abdur-Razzaq Lubis. 2011. *Kinta Valley: Pioneering Malaysia's Modern Development*. Ipoh, Malaysia: Perak Academy.

Kratoska, Paul H. 2001. *South East Asia, Colonial History: Empire-building in the nineteenth century*. London: Routledge.

Kuper, Adam. 1980. *Anthropology and Anthropologists: The British School in the twentieth century*. New York: Routledge.

Lockwood, Rupert. 1951. *Malaya must cost no more Australian blood*. Sydney: Current Book Distributors.

Loh Kok-Wah, Francis. 1988. *Beyond the Tin Mines: coolies, squatters, and New Villagers in the Kinta Valley, Malaysia, c. 1880–1980*. Singapore: Oxford University Press.

Lynn, Martin. 1999. British policy, trade and informal Empire in the mid-nineteenth century. In *The Oxford History of the British Empire: Volume III: The Nineteenth Century*, edited by A. Porter. New York: Oxford University Press.

Mao Tse-tung. 1968. 'On Guerrilla Warfare'. In *Selected Works*, vol. IX. Peking: Foreign Languages Press.

———. 1968. Report on an Investigation of the Peasant Movement in Hunan. In *Selected Works*, vol. I. Peking: Foreign Languages Press.

Marx, Karl. *The Eighteenth Brumaire of Louis Bonaparte*. Moscow: Progress Press. (1937 edn).

———. *The German Ideology*. Moscow: Progress Press. (1964 edn).

Marx, Karl, Frederick Engels. *The Communist Manifesto*. New York: International Publishers, (1948 edn).

Mockatitis, Thomas R. 2012. 'The minimum force debate: contemporary sensibilities meet imperial practice.' *Small Wars & Insurgencies* 23 (4–5): 762–80.

Nyce, Ray. 1973. *Chinese New Vllages in Malaya; a community study*. Singapore: Malaysian Sociological Research Institute.

Orwell, George. 1968. Shooting an Elephant. In *The Collected Essays, Journalism and Letters of George Orwell, vol. 1*. Harmondsworth, England: Penguin.

Peng, Chin and Ian Ward. 2005. *My Side of History*. Singapore: Media Master.

Porter, Bernard. 2007. 'Trying to make decolonisation look good.' *London Review of Books* 29 (15): 6–10.

Purcell, Victor. 1955. *Malaya. Communist or free*. Stanford: Stanford University Press.

——. 1965. *Malaysia*. London: Thames and Hudson.

——. 1967. *The Chinese in Malaya*, Kuala Lumpur: Oxford University Press.

Ramakrishna, Kumar. 2001. '"Transmogrifying" Malaya; The impact of Sir Gerald Templer (1952–54)'. *Journal of Southeast Asian Studies* 32 (2): 79–92.

——. 2002. '"Bribing the Reds to give up": Rewards policy in the Malayan Emergency'. *War in History* 9 (3): 332–53.

——. 2002. *Emergency Propaganda: The Winning of Malayan Hearts and Minds, 1948–1958*. London: Curzon.

Renick, R.D. 1965. 'The Emergency Regulations of Malaya: Causes and Effects'. *Journal of Southeast Asian History* 6 (2): 1–39.

Rostow, W.W. 1960. *The Stages of Economic Growth: A Non-Communist Manifesto*. Cambridge: Cambridge University Press.

Royle, Trevor. 2010. *Orde Wingate: A Man of Genius 1903–1944*. London: Frontline Books.

Said, Edward W. 1994. *Culture and Imperialism*. London: Vintage.

——. 2003. Always on top. *London Review of Books* 25 (6): 3–6.

Sandhu, Kernal Singh. 1964. 'The saga of the "squatter" in Malaya'. *Journal of Southeast Asian Studies* 5 (1): 145–77.

Sartre, Jean-Paul, 1963. 'Introduction.' In Frantz Fanon: *Wretched of the Earth*. New York: Grove Press.

Schenk, Catherine R. 1994. *Britain and the Sterling Area: From Devaluation to Convertibility in the 1950s*. London: Routledge.

Short, Anthony. 1970. 'Race and politics in Malaysia.' *Asian Survey* 10 (12): 1081–89.

——. 1975. *The Communist Insurrection in Malaya 1948–1960*. London: Frederick Muller.

Schwarcz, Vera. 1986. *The Chinese Enlightenment : intellectuals and the legacy of the May Fourth movement of 1919*. Berkeley: University of California Press.

Spence, Jonathan D. 1981. *The Gate of Heavenly Peace: the Chinese and their revolution, 1895–1980*. New York: Viking Press.

Srinivasan, Krishnan. 2005. *The Rise, Decline and Future of the British Commonwealth*. London: Palgrave Macmillan.

Stalin, Joseph. 1954. 'Marxism and the National Question.' In *Works*. Moscow: Foreign Languages Publishing House.

Steward, Brian. 2004. *Smashing Terrorism in the Malayan Emergency*. Kuala Lumpur: Pelanduk Publications.

Stubbs, Richard. 1989. *Hearts and Minds in Guerrilla Warfare: the Malayan Emergency 1948–1960*. Singapore: Oxford University Press.

Tan Jing Quee and Jomo K.S. (eds). 2001. *Comet in the Sky: Lim Chin Siong in History*. Kuala Lumpur: ISAN.

Tan Ten-Phee. 2009. "'Like a Concentration Camp, lah'": Chinese grassroots experience of the Emergency and new villages in British Colonial Malaya.' *Chinese Southern Diaspora Studies* 3: 216–28.

Thatcher, Dorothy and Robert Cross. 1959. *Pai Naa: the Story of Nona Baker*. London: Constable.

Thornton, Rod. 2004. 'The British Army and the origin of its minimum force philosopy.' *Small Wars & Insurgencies* 15 (1): 83–106.

Tilman, Robert O. 1966. 'The non-lessons of the Malayan Emergency.' *Asian Survey* 6 (8): 407–19.

Townshend, Charles. 2005. 'People's War.' In *The Oxford History of Modern War*, edited by C. Townshend. Oxford: Oxford University Press.

United States Dept. of the Army. 2007. *The U.S. Army/Marine Corps Counterinsurgency Field Manual* Chicago: University of Chicago Press.

Wakeman, Frederic, Jr. 2007. *The Fall of Imperial China*. New York: Free Press.

Walley, Christine J. 2013. *Exit Zero: Family and Class in Postindustrial Chicago*. Chicago: University of Chicago Press.

Wasserstrom, C. K and E.J. Perry. 1994. *Popular Protest and Political Culture in Modern China*. Boulder, Colorado: Westview Press.

White, Nicholas J. 1998. 'Capitalism and counter-insurgency? Business and government in the Malayan Emergency, 1948–57.' *Modern Asian Studies* 32 (1): 149–77.

Whittingham, Daniel. 2012. "'Savage warfare": C.E. Callwell, the roots of counterinsurgency, and the nineteenth century context.' *Small Wars & Insurgencies* 23 (4–5): 591–607.

Yong, C.F. 1991. 'Origins and development of the Malayan Communist Movement, 1919–1939.' *Modern Asian History* 25 (4): 625–48.

———. 1997. *The Origin of Malayan Communism*. Singapore: South Sea Society.

Index

Maps and illustrations indicated by **bold** entries.

early British response, 43–50, 81
'ethnic Chinese factor', 119–121
legacy, 59, 164, 166
measures against insurgency. See
    Emergency Regulations; 'hearts
    and minds'; resettlement
memory and understanding of,
    22–25, 33, 41, 42, 77, 95, 123, 134,
    154, 157, 158
victor's narrative, 41
'white areas', 112
see also Malayan Communist Party;
    Malayan National Liberation Army;
    military violence
Malayan communism
and Chinese nationalism, 26–27
influence of May Fourth Movement,
    27
and progressive literature, 34–37
and second Sino-Japanese War
    (1937–45), 27, 119
see also Malayan Left
Malayan Communist Party (MCP)
1989 peace agreement with Malaysia
    and Thailand, 20, 31, 60, 123
alliances with Malay and Malayan-
    Indian communists, 121–124. See
    also Malay communists; Malayan
    Indians: communists
internal purge, 159
leadership. See CD Abdullah; Chin
    Peng; Lai Teck
'Long March' to Betong, 62
mainly Chinese membership, 124
Min Yuen teams, 24, 25, 108, 112
and the 'National Question', 126–127,
    132
origin and history, 26, 29–30
protection of Chinese interests, 120
reminiscences of ex-MCP insurgents,
    22–25, 31–38
uneasy peace with the British, 42-43
united front politics, 31, 42, 61,
    62–63

see also Malayan People's
    Anti-Japanese Army (MPAJA),
    Malayan National Liberation Army
    (MNLA)
Malayan Indian Congress, 75, 92–93,
    163. See also Malayan Chinese Associa-
    tion; UMNO
Malayan Indians, 129, 140
in civil service, 92
communists, 121, 123–124, 132, 139.
    See also Balan; Ganapathy; MCP;
    Veerasenan
community, 92
deportation, 28, 56
in government. See Malayan Indian
    Congress
granting of citizenship and constitu-
    tional rights, 92
labourers, 7, 28, 127
Malayan Left
and British return, 30–31
cosmopolitanism, 131–132
early history, 28–29
inspiration of the Bandung Confer-
    ence, 131
and 'leftist literature', 34–37
and the MCP, 131
see also Lim Chin Siong, Malay
    Nationalism, 'Malayan Spring'
Malayan National Liberation Army
    (MNLA), **24, 44, 45, 49**, 54, 60, **71**,
    73, 160, 165
beginning of insurgency, 40–41
British counter-measures. See
    Malayan Emergency
change in military strategy, 90, 104
early successes against British, 43–50,
    81, 99–100
failure of insurgency, 14, 90, 96, 121,
    134, 162
Maoist strategy. See Mao Tse-tung;
    revolutionary war
origins. See Malayan People's
    Anti-Japanese Army

Raffles, Sir Thomas Stamford, 9–10
resettlement, **54, 58**
  Briggs' Plan, 53–54, 86–87, 99, 100,
    107. See also Briggs
  and counter-insurgency, 55
  and Emergency Regulations, 55–58
  figures of people deported, 56, 57
  and regrouping, 97
  role of MCA, 108
  Templer and, 87
  see also New Villages
revolutionary war, 73, 94
  in China, 62. See also Mao Tse-tung
  failure of Malayan ~ , 75–76
  retreat to the countryside, 62
  revolutionary potential of peasants, 69
  see also Marx/Marxism
rubber
  export earnings, 15
  and commodity fetishism, 16–18
  history of industry, 6–7

Said, Edward, 162, 173,
Selangor, **ix**, 6, 8, 25, 36, 54, **99**, 109
Singapore, **ix**, 6–10 *passim*, 21, 23, 30, 33,
  34, 63, **99**, 119, 122, 123, 124, 131, 132,
  134, 141, 146–148, 161–162. *See also*
  Malaya: Straits Settlements; Malaysia
Soviet Union, viii, 4, 5, 126, 127, 133,
  139, 140, 165
  blamed for insurgency, 4
  Stalin and the 'National Question',
    125–26
Special Branch, 24, 41, 70, 78, 89
squatters. *See* Kinta Valley
sterling area, 12–14. *See also* British
  Empire; gold standard
sultans. *See* Malaya
Sungei Siput. *See* Elphil Estate killing
Sungei Lembing, 137, 141, 142. *See also*
  Baker

Tan Cheng Lock (Dato Sir Cheng Lock
  Tan), 92, 93. *See also* Malayan Chinese
  Association
Tanjong Malim, **ix**, 109, 110, 111, 147, 148

'technique', 109–110, 110, 111
  see also collective punishment; Templer
Templer, Field Marshal Sir Gerald, **80**
  appointed High Commissioner and
    Director of Operations, 53, 81
  and British art of counter-insurgency,
    83–85
  and collective punishment, 109–111.
    See also collective punishment
  'hearts and minds' approach, 81,
    85–87, 91. See also 'hearts and minds'
  leadership, 81–83, 87–88
  military career, pre-Malaya, 80
  and political reform, 92–94
  and the 'Tanjong Malim technique',
    109–110
tin
  and commodity fetishism, 16–18
  export earnings, 16
  history of, 6
Trengganu, **ix, 99**

Union of Malay Youth (KMM), 116,
  128–130. *See also* CD Abdullah;
  Mustapha Hussain, Malay nationalism
United Malay National Organization
  (UMNO), 129
  alliance with MCA, 92–93, 108
  founding, 92
  see also Malayan Chinese Associa-
    tion; Malayan Indian Congress;
    Mustapha Hussain

United States, 5, 14, 44, 49
  denies support for British in
    Emergency, 6
  counter-insurgency, 51, 94, 104
  economic power, 12, 13, 103
  resentment of Empire, 5
  role in Cold War, 5, 15

Veerasenan, P., 124. *See also* Malayan
  Indians: communists

Wavell, Field Marshal Earl
  on 'British warriors', 150–151
  on Chapman, 150